THEFT AND DRUGS IN THE WORK PLACE

by K. C. BETTENCOURT

Published by

R&E Publishers

P.O. Box 2008
Saratoga, CA 95070
Phone: (408) 866-6303
Fax: (408) 866-0825

I.S.B.N. 0-88247-852-4

LC-90-63054

For information: K.C. Bettencourt, 999 C Edgewater Drive, Suite 253, Foster City, CA 94404

THEFT & DRUGS IN THE WORKPLACE

CONTENTS

Introduction

Because the mention of alcohol usage is not a major part of this book, does not mean it is condoned in the workplace. Alcohol is a major contributor of all traffic fatalities and is still legal. But in almost every case, the drunk driver is slapped on the wrist and it is the victims who are left grieving over the death of a loved one.

According to the American Institute of Criminology and Research, in most cases, it is the combination of drugs and alcohol that causes the highest rate of accidents on our nation's highways.

Entertaining clients over a three-martini lunch has become an accepted way of doing business in Silicon Valley. And let us not forget the parties given for the benefit of existing clients. But if an account representative fails to go along with the program he or she is looked down upon. What is forgotten is that an employer is libel if an employee should have an accident leaving one of these functions.

In my opinion, just because alcohol consumption is legal does not make it right. If legalization of some drugs are made, if would be a matter of time when drug consumption, like alcohol, will become an accepted way of doing business within the workplace.

Dedicated to M.A.D.D.

(Mothers Against Drunk Drivers)

CHAPTER ONE

Introduction to Loss Prevention

Internal Theft Study

Research by the National Institute of Justice concluded that it is company policy, rather than sophisticated security operations, that can be the greatest deterrent to employee misconduct. Where employees feel that the organization has their best interests at heart, employee theft is likely to be low.

Those companies with a clear policy on theft, inventory control with theft reduction as a major priority, and pre-employment screening procedures had lower levels of employee theft. Also, where the work force apprehensions for theft were higher, the overall theft rates were lower.

Overview of the Problem Nationally

Estimates by the Department of Commerce in 1976 placed the total inventory loss attributable to employee theft at $30 billion. Such losses were projected to increase by 35 percent every five years.

Existing Employee Theft Research

American Institute of Criminology and Research reviewed the historical development of pilferage by employees in 1977 and concluded that those "wages in kind" have, over time, become an important part of the employee's wage structure.

A survey of 100 retail employees confirmed that most employees do not view theft from the company as stealing, despite the contrary opinions held by their employers. They also found that 41 of 49 employees who admitted taking from their companies denied any feelings of guilt. Statements by dishonest employees were along the lines that "everyone does it," "no one cares if you take a few things," "these items are not of significant value," and so on.

The National Retail Association warned in 1956 that there is not a direct relationship between organizational size and stealing; factors associated with larger companies, like "anonymity, impersonality, bureaucratic inefficiency, and power," seem to influence the decision to victimize a business organization.

The National Retail Association concluded in its 1972 study that employee theft results from inevitable conflicts between organizational demands and workers' perceptions.

Employee Deviance

Theoretical similarity between employee theft of money or merchandise should also extend to lunch and coffee breaks, work slowdowns, absenteeism, and inferior workmanship.

Occasional and systematic deviance by employees has been discovered by social science researchers within a variety of occupations and organizations. The available research documenting both acts against the property of the work organization (that is, employee theft) and the expected level of productivity (that is, counterproductive behavior) generally suggests uniform conclusions. First, the roots of deviant behavior, which may be detrimental to the interest of the employer, are to a great extent an integral part of the informal work experience. Factors that best explain these behaviors are not external to the work setting, but rather are intrinsically related to the nature of the employment setting.

The second conclusion is that the employee's perception of the quality of the work environment has a significant effect on the decision to become involved in theft and other forms of counter-productive behavior.

Employee theft and behavior are generally not random events. Rather, they represent a purposeful response to the social and environmental factors present in the work setting.

Prevalence of Property Theft and Production Deviance

Most employees, according to a survey reported by the National Institute of Justice in 1983, have "no involvement" in theft. Involvement in theft in the range of "a half dozen or so items" was admitted by 35 percent of employees surveyed. In retail stores, the most commonly reported category of property theft was the unauthorized use of employee discount privileges. Misuse of this fringe benefit within the preceding year was admitted by 29 percent of respondents. Of these, 14 percent admitted abusing this privilege on a monthly or more frequent basis. Other types of theft were also reported: 7 percent admitted taking store merchandise; 3 percent reported that they had taken cash (see tables 1 and 2).

Policy Implications

To the extent that the organization's structure and processes themselves produce both property and production deviance, corporate actions to modify in some fashion any of the included behaviors and reaction to it should be informed of the full content of the general category it is dealing with. The close relationship between property deviance and other types of counter-productive behavior suggests that these phenomena may be dealt with theoretically as all parts of the same generic behavior systems. That is, they are violations of relatively dynamic organizational rules. Being permissive on some specific types of property and/or production deviance can also signal permissiveness on others, unless careful attention is given to defining what is included and what is excluded from the definition.

Research findings caution in the development of programs which attempted to control property and/or production deviance. Testimony of employees indicated that many, perhaps most, do not see themselves as involved in theft from the company. To design control programs that would in effect "accuse" employees of theft prior to addressing the definitional issue of what is and what is not theft, runs the risk of initiating considerable resentment perhaps of sufficient strength to bring about increased employee deviance rather than less of it. The vast majority of employees do not see themselves as thieves or disloyal, even though they might take company property. The reaction by employees in the event a law enforcement would be used to respond to the above-described deviances would likely be to raise a series of undesirable issues.

External Economic Pressures and Theft

Employee theft has been treated as a street crime. Unfortunately, understanding what causes street crime does not help in understanding employee theft. Employees who take from the company do not seem to be grossly impoverished, nor are they in precarious financial situations that might entice them to steal.

Employee theft should be viewed as an "internal crime problem" that may be unrelated to the level of conventional crime in the surrounding community.

Policy Implications

Researchers suggest that employers should not continue to treat employee theft as a traditional law enforcement problem. Employee theft (particularly the pilferage variety) seems to be a manifestation of deviance, largely violating the rules of the organization, not the norms of society. People who are not thieves by nature may take from the company and not define their behavior as theft. To understand employee theft, we must examine factors that take into consideration the social variables of the work place, not the factors of the metropolitan area.

The Younger Employee and Theft

Younger employees (16 to mid-20s) reported more employee theft than their older coworkers. Younger, short-tenured, unmarried male employees produce images of an entire generation of workers who do not have the same respect for property as their older coworkers. It is not known, however, whether these younger employees are indeed any more or less deviant than more senior workers were when they were young.

If employees are allowed to believe that they had no personal involvement in the success of the organization, theft from the organization becomes much more easy to justify or neutralize (American Institute of Criminology and Research). Employees who are young and unmarried may simply be less deterrable because they have minimal stakes in conforming compared to their older, married colleagues (American Institute of Criminology and Research). To younger employees, the loss of employment and subsequent embarrassment in front of family and coworkers as a punishment for theft does not carry the same social risks it does for older employees.

Policy Implications

If an organization expects to reduce theft problems by weeding out employee thieves one by one, the procedure will be expensive and time-consuming. Achieving general deterrence to theft will require:

1. Prosecution
2. Consistently prosecuting
3. Communicating the fact of prosecutions to other workers

If any worker can easily infer (especially any young worker) that he or she is being exploited (that is, denied promotional advantages, wages, supervisors, and so on), the climate is ripe for deviance and theft. It has long been known that blocked channels of opportunity can provide the impetus to street crime (American Institute of Criminology and

Research). Now, there is evidence that this situation may influence the occurrence of criminal behavior in the work place, as well.

Job Dissatisfaction and Property and Production Deviance

For the most part, gathered data indicates disgruntled employees would be involved in greater theft and production deviance than satisfied employees. Where the integrity, fairness, and ethical quality of the organization is questioned, more theft is found. Where the supervisory personnel are perceived as unhelpful, incompetent, and unconcerned, higher theft is detected.

Policy Implications

The employees' perception of first-line supervisory personnel appears to be the critical element in understanding the occurrence of employee deviance. The interpersonal and management skills which supervisors possess can have a profound effect on the attitudes of their subordinates. When work supervisors are not responsive to the needs of their employees, they can aggravate the deviance situation by providing a personal focus to the victimization.

While not all of these factors may be easily controllable, many, such as competence of supervisors, adequacy of communication, fairness in employee-employer relations, recognition of quality performance, ethical behavior on the part of higher management, and so on, are probably most responsive to organizational attention.

Organizational Controls and Employee Theft

The analysis reveals that organizational controls do indeed have an effect on the prevalence of property-taking with a company.

There is consistent evidence that those companies with a clearly defined and promulgated anti-theft policy have lower theft levels.

Repeatedly announcing to the work force that employee theft will not be permitted at any level can lower theft rates, particularly if emphasis is placed on other controls as well (such as visible negative sanctions to back up policy). This study suggests that management must clearly convey via word and deed that taking property is not acceptable behavior within the organization.

If individuals with inventory control responsibilities make a conscious effort to monitor usage patterns, watch for irregularities and then check into why this may be occurring. The organization conveys that it is concerned about its property and its use. The data also suggests that pre-employment screening of prospective employees is a modestly effective theft control strategy.

The higher proportion of apprehension for theft, the lower the theft rate. The eventual outcome did not seem to have a direct deterrent effect.

Policy Implications

Those firms that signal to their employees that taking company property and assets will be viewed as theft, that establish rules and procedures to detect theft of property by employees, and further, are selective about whom they choose to employ, generally are found to have lower levels of theft by employees.

First, line supervisors inherit both the latitude and responsibility for effecting a control environment that facilitates (or at least does not significantly impede) the basic production process.

Employee theft cannot be ignored or relegated to a topic of temporary or minimal importance, nor should it be assigned as a task for a specialized portion of the organizations management team. This research suggests that only by exhibiting a conspicuous and consistent climate of concern about controlling internal theft at all occupational levels can an organization hope to have a significant effect on the behavior of its employees.

The Process of Defining Property and Production Deviance in the Work Place

Deviance in the work place are not perceived by employees to be conventional theft. "What is Deviant" and "From Whose Perspective" become very problematic questions. Thus it is possible for acts that are defined as deviant by management not to be so labelled by the worker's fellow workers.

Policy Implications

It would seem apparent that significant intervention into current operational definitions and reactions to theft and time deviance would require organization-wide clarification of acceptable and unacceptable production activities and supervisory relationships. Adequate accountability procedures would remove from the "grey area" much of the substance that now fuels the "negotiation of deviance" process. Unless extreme care were used, such changes would be made at some cost to supervisory "resources" and employee "perks" at all levels of the organization. Any revamping of expectations of employee behavior should be accompanied by sufficient initial and continuous training and information dissemination to ensure employee awareness and understanding. Rewards for observance of newly agreed-upon rules should be evident and consistent.

THEFT DETECTION FLOW CHART

Product Loss (Table 1)

Indicators	Department Monitoring	Correct Response	Correct Action
Unusual reorder quantities	Order service	Contact supervisor the person ordering reports to.	Supervisor reviews order, determines appropriateness, negative findings reported to loss prevention.
New Releases missing over-night	Store management	Ask employee to recall volume sold	Try to recall suspicious persons, write incident report, send to loss prevention.
Shipment over/short, number of	Store management	Call distribution center, loss prevention Ext: (if applies)	Do not keep extra cartons, locate missing cartons.
Purchase discount greater than reasonable	Store management loss prevention	Ask employee to explain	Store management contact loss prevention if explanation not appropriate.

THEFT DETECTION FLOW CHART

Product Loss (Table 2)

Indicators	Department Monitoring	Correct Response	Correct Action
Mark-down percentage out of line with the normal	Store management, district manager, regional L/P Manager, accounting	Identify the employee working the register and take corrective action	Observe—spot audit the drawer - test shop the O/A, interview.
Dollar amount paid larger than scheduled hours worked	Store management District managers Regional managers	Each pay period store management compare amount paid against scheduled hours, district mgr. spot check stores in their district	Notify payroll of irregularities and loss prevention of corrective action taken if improprieties exist.
Long lunch or breaks	Store management District managers Regional managers	Interview	Counseling report termination
Arrive late/leave early	Store management District managers Regional managers	Interview	Counseling report termination
Work under the influence of drugs or alcohol	Store management District managers Regional managers Loss prevention	Interview	Counseling report termination Prosecution if drugs are found

CHAPTER TWO

Loss Prevention Information

Introduction to Loss Prevention

Loss prevention is "the prevention of loss before it occurs." It is something that, if not used, can cost companies millions of dollars. Loss prevention is the safest, easiest, cheapest and most effective way to decrease loss caused by theft and, thereby, *increase profits.*

Loss Prevention Is Your Responsibility!

When and Where Does It Apply?

In our personal lives or at work, loss prevention applies from the time we lock our homes before going to work, to the time we lock our stores when we leave work.

It applies when we put money in our wallets or purses and when we put a cash drop in the safe. We all use loss prevention every day of our lives.

Is it better to catch a burglar in your home, or to lock the door and prevent the entry? By locking the door, you use a loss prevention technique at home.

Is it better to watch a shoplifter conceal merchandise, or to wait upon that person before the merchandise is concealed? Customer service is one of our most effective loss prevention techniques.

Loss prevention can be used in nearly every job assignment. Let's look at a few assignments and see what type of prevention occurs if attention is applied to preventing losses.

Assignment	**Type of Prevention**
1. Customer service	Shoplifting prevention
2. Bag sealing	Shoplifter prevention
3. Stock maintenance	Booster/shoplifting prevention
4. Displays/merchandising	Booster/shoplifting prevention
5. Hiring/interviewing/screening	Dishonesty/risk prevention
6. Training	Mistake/error prevention
7. Reconciliation	Cash theft/error prevention
8. Locking the cash drawer	Till tap prevention
9. Checking identification	Check/charge fraud prevention
10. Count back change	Short change artist prevention
11. Morning deposits	Robbery prevention
12. Money locked in safe	Robbery Prevention
13. Setting the alarm	Burglary prevention
14. Locking the door	Burglary prevention
15. Training	Internal theft prevention
16. Reacting to losses	Internal theft prevention
17. Building relationships	Internal theft prevention

Responsibility

Loss prevention is everyone's responsibility. As employees, the company belongs to everyone; if the company loses, we all lose. The losses are in the form of lost pay raises, bonuses, company growth, new positions, higher prices, lower stock prices, and so on. Imagine the effectiveness of a loss prevention team that has all employees working together.

The battle against shrinkage is the "company team" together as employees against individuals who steal through internal or external means, and against careless paperwork and loose controls.

Terminology

The following terms are used throughout this manual. Knowing them will help you understand loss prevention and the role each term represents in protecting your company's assets.

1. ***Booster*** A person who steals large quantities. A booster often steals with accomplices. ***Booster setup*** A large quantity of product(s) concealed by a booster before a theft.
2. ***Counterfeit*** v. To copy without authority, to forge, to imitate with intent to deceive. n. An imitation, forgery.
3. ***External*** Theft or loss caused by someone not employed by the company.
4. ***Fraud*** Theft by using false documents, falsifying documents, or forgery.
5. ***Internal*** Theft caused by an employee of the company.

6. ***Prevention*** Doing something to avoid loss. Keeping someone from doing something that might cause loss. Anticipating and countering in advance.
7. ***Profit*** The money the company makes after all expenses and losses are deducted. If the company profits, all employees profit, and the company's stock value increases.
8. ***Shrink*** The amount of loss the company sustains as a result of theft and errors.

Statistics

Retail shrinkage in the United States exceeds $50 billion annually. Shrinkage breaks down into three categories. An estimated percentage of shrinkage is as follows:

Internal	50 to 60 percent
External	10 to 20 percent
Errors	10 to 20 percent

Profit Margin Breakdown--The Cost of Shrinkage

When a loss occurs, it's important to know how much we really lose and what it costs. Look at the following examples:

A $100 loss represents--

$40 in product cost

$10 in payroll

$10 in construction

$10 in rent and utilities

$ 6 in signs and advertising

$10 in miscellaneous operating costs

$10 in equipment and data processing

$ 4 in net profit

If, as indicated here, the company makes only $4 profit on $100 of sales, a loss or theft of $100 must be deducted directly from the company's net profits. Making up for such a loss requires 25 $100 transactions at $4 net profit per transaction, to cover a $100 loss. This means $2500 of product must be sold to cover a $100 loss or theft.

A $10 loss or cash shortage really costs the company $250.

A $1 loss or cash shortage really costs the company $25.

Any employee who dishonestly fails to charge a $1 rental fee or marks down an item $1 for a friend costs everyone who is part of the company $25!

Loss Prevention Standards

The following standards constitute a model for the regulations of any company's loss prevention policies.

Step 1. All current employees must read these standards. New employees must read them on their first day of employment.

Step 2. After the employees read the standards, company management must explain each loss prevention standard to new employees on their first day of employment, and must answer all questions. Then, the employee must sign the loss prevention sign-off form that follows.

The loss prevention standards, as established, should be posted in the area of each location where employees report for work.

Remember: Violation of any of these standards can lead to termination or dismissal from the company. The management is to review these standards with the entire crew at every meeting.

Management's Responsibility

Management is responsible for seeing that all standards are adhered to. On reading and understanding the Loss Prevention Standards, each employee must complete the compliance agreement and place it in the new-hire "priority" envelope.

Documentation

Documentation is an important tool in all aspects of the company. Properly documenting an incident can make a big difference in various cases. For example:

- A successful apprehension and prosecution, or a defense of the company and any of its employees who are the targets of civil lawsuits.
- Preventing false unemployment or Labor Board claims that could cause the company financial loss.
- Correctly filling out and submitting proper documents on shoplifting apprehension assures restitution to the company of at least $150 through civil damages.

Review the following report forms and know when and how to use each of them.

Statement of Fact

Your company can obtain copies of these forms from the American Institute of Criminology and Research. This form is used only when a person (internal or external) causes a loss and is detained or apprehended. It is to be filled out immediately following an incident involving an apprehension. This form protects the company in legal situations and insures it at least $150 in civil damages. This form should always be accompanied by an Incident Report and Apprehension Report if shoplifting was involved. It is to be forwarded to Loss Prevention in an envelope labelled "Loss Prevention—Attn: Statement of Fact."

Incident Report

The Incident Report is the most versatile report form. It is used for any incident that may occur. Fill it out for *all* Loss Prevention incidents, including:

- Alarm Reports
- Robberies
- Shoplifting
- Information Only
- Property Damage
- Accidents
- Booster
- Customer Incident/Threat
- Associate Incident
- Missing Product
- Burglary
- Check/Charge Fraud
- Short Change
- Till Tap
- Drug/Alcohol Incidents
- Discovery of Peeled Sensormatic Tags or Shrinkwraps

Forward this report in an envelope marked "Loss Prevention—Attn. Incident Report."

Employee Written Statement

This is a memo that an employee fills out to verify any verbal statement. This protects by allowing any associate involved to verify in writing that verbal speech occurred. It also protects against false statements. This document is used for cases of dishonesty, resignations, suspensions, and so on, and will be used to protect the company should the need arise. Use a three-part memo or other paper with copies. Any employee who makes an admission of theft, dishonesty, or policy violation *should* be asked to document such admission on a written statement.

Apprehension Report

If a thief or shoplifter is apprehended, complete the following apprehension report and send it with all incident reports filed on this instance to "Loss Prevention—Attn: Incident Report."

Careline

The Careline flyer will be posted in all stores. Careline, an independent outside agency, can be used by an employee or customer. When using Careline, you always have the option of remaining anonymous. When you call, any information, problems, or comments you make will remain strictly confidential.

You can use Careline for any of the following reasons:

- To make a complaint
- To report a problem in your store or within the company
- To report suspicious activities or concerns
- To report dishonesty

Your input will be given to the person or department in the company best suited to address and confidentially resolve the problem. Any additional information you may want to report pertaining to your original call can be phoned into Careline at any time.

Using information given to Careline by you and other associates will enable the company to respond to matters that might otherwise go unnoticed. Post the Careline poster in clear view for employees and customers and show it to all new hires during the store tour.

Internal Theft

Preventing loss resulting from **dishonesty** is one of your major tasks. Reporting that theft can prevent that loss and similar losses in the future. Honest employees working as a team against dishonesty will ensure a safe, comfortable and profitable environment in which to work and grow. Reducing internal theft will also increase the number of individuals successfully promoted to management positions. Minor violations too often affect individual career development. Don't allow dishonesty to ruin your career or your chance for promotion.

Types of internal theft/dishonesty

Cash theft

Theft of cash from the company:

- Registers
- Cash drawers
- Safe
- Deposits
- Drops
- Petty cash
- Paychecks
- Personal property
- Rental transactions
- Non-rings
- Deletions
- Voids
- Credit slips
- Gift Certificates
- Markdowns
- BASS (if applies)
- Borrowing funds
- Cashing personal checks
- Merchandise
- Transportation

Product theft

Theft of salable or unsalable product from the company:

- Borrowing product
- Giving away product
- Destroying product
- Allowing theft
- Unauthorized markdowns
- Deletions

Fraud

Filling out any company documents with false or fraudulent information:

- Applications
- Credit slips
- Gift certificates
- Receipts
- Checks
- Credit card drafts
- Sales drafts
- Petty cash forms
- Time/pay sheets
- Transactions
- Receiving logs
- Forfeitures
- Purchase orders
- Falsification of any signature
- Daily closing envelope
- Physical inventory forms
- Misticketing/mispricing

Miscellaneous

Removal, destruction, or unauthorized use of company:

- Fixtures
- Supplies or materials
- Equipment
- Allowing any type of theft or loss to occur
- Accepting gratuities, kickbacks, or unauthorized gifts from customers

CHAPTER THREE

Indicators and Prevention of Internal Dishonesty

Certain indicators give advance warning that problems exist either in the form of errors or dishonesty. Along with the company's accounting and auditing departments which track and control losses, it's vital that managers in the field learn to recognize some of the potential problems and be able to react to them at the store level.

Watch for these internal problem indicators:

- violations of company policies seemingly on purpose or on a regular basis
- frequent tardiness and absenteeism
- an overall poor attitude and constant complaints
- inventory shrinkages or losses (don't always assume that these are a result of shoplifting or the work of boosters)
- frequent customer complaints about certain employees
- products concealed in areas accessible only to employees
- reductions in sales in conjunction with increased product orders
- unusual patterns or increases in cash overages and shortages concerning the same employee
- reported cash-overages and shortage discrepancies compared with actual audit figures

- voids, credit slips, or gift certificates that are not approved
- register tickets withheld or concealed
- unauthorized signing of documents
- consistently lower net sales on a shift for one employee compared with other employees working the same shift
- frequent mistakes leading to cash or product losses
- unusual requests, such as offers to take out trash, always operate a cash drawer or work in one station
- continual confusion on the part of an employee that may lead to losses resulting from errors
- missing detail tapes, checks, charges, or other documents
- products appearing to be missing but not sold (as determined by checking inventory against detail tapes/register tapes)
- excessive overages or shortages in store audit or close out procedures
- excessive security violations in the store
- excessive markdown amounts
- failure to follow company purchase policies

Opportunity

Opportunity is a major cause of internal loss. This can be controlled when management is closely supervising and monitoring the staff. It's important to note that usually the person with the most opportunity should be the person who can be trusted the most and supervised the least. Most often individuals with opportunity (along with need and the desire) fall into acts of dishonesty.

Procedures to Prevent and Reduce Internal Theft

- post loss prevention standards. Enforce them all, and set an example by following them
- lock the safe
- institute individual cash drawer reconciliation
- conduct "spot audits" daily
- verify cash drops with a second sign off
- verify inventory counts
- follow employees
- return to the selling floor any product found concealed in the store. In addition, ask all employees if they were aware of the product concealed in that location. Complete an Incident Report.
- never let the store be closed by one person alone; always have two or more close together
- designate a safe location inside the store for personal belongings of employees. If there is no such space available, instruct employees not to bring personal property into the store.
- don't let anyone use your keys or have access to your keys

Indicator and Prevention Examples

Effectively preventing internal theft is accomplished by combining these elements:

- setting clear expectations and standards
- assuring management and employee knowledge of causes of dishonesty

- recognizing problem indicators
- using prevention techniques to reduce and eliminate opportunity
- communicating to all employees any and all losses or discovery of possible losses and what employees can do to help
- using and inspecting a nightly loss prevention awareness report and confronting employees who have questionable transactions and patterns

Cash Theft and Prevention Examples

Here are types of internal cash thefts, their indicators, and how to prevent them.

Outright/Direct Cash Theft from the Cash Drawer

- *indicators:* excessive shortages, patterns of shortages, even dollar amount shortages ($5, $10, $20, and so on), unusual transaction or unusual patterns noted on the loss prevention awareness report
- *prevention:* institute individual cash drawer reconciliation procedure. This will reduce opportunity by limiting the cash drawer to one associate per shift. Shortages can then be isolated to the employee causing them.

Producing Fraudulent Voids, Credits and Gift Certificates, Use of Markdown

- *indicators:* falsified signature, incomplete information, no management approval, documents created when management is not present, excessive markdown percentages, unusual transactions found on the loss prevention awareness report.

- *prevention:* require management approval for all voids, credits, and certificates at the time of their occurrence or issuance in the customer's presence. If management is not in the store, an employee should be designated to stand in to witness and sign off transactions

Failure to Ring (or Void) Sales

- *indicators:* overage and shortage patterns; complaints from customers of not receiving register tickets; employee continually failing to have voids approved at the time of their occurrence; register tickets being saved at the work station; products missing but not sold (not on the detail tape); deleted transactions on the loss prevention awareness report.
- *prevention:* institute the individual cash drawer reconciliation procedure and monitor over/short patterns; make all employees aware of patterns and/or customer complaints of not receiving register tickets; monitor all employees who fail to have voids immediately approved or who save register tickets.

Theft of Rental Income

- *indicators:* altered fees or charges on register tickets; discovery of destroyed register tickets; appearance of transactions on register loss prevention reports.
- *prevention:* spot-check register tickets for correct amount of charge; monitor sales areas for lost or destroyed receipts, research all register loss prevention reports and question employees whose names appear frequently on the reports; have management only approve no-charges for return of defective rental merchandise.

Outright Cash Theft from Safe, Banks, Drops, Deposit, or Petty Cash

- *indicators:* safe shortages, nightly shortages or petty cash shortages that don't show up on audits
- *prevention:* limit access to safe and keys to management only

Cash Theft from Employee Drawers

- *indicators:* unexplained shortages, missing negotiables
- *prevention:* as per audit procedure, let only one employee have access to only one drawer per assignment; remove keys and lock cash drawer when employees are away from their cash drawer or when their cash drawer is not in use

Theft from Personal Belongings, Purses

- *indicators:* employees report loss(es)
- *prevention:* designate a "safe" area for employee belongings that is out of customer view and reach, and which can be watched, locked or secured by management

Deletion of Transactions

- *indicators:* register loss prevention awareness report shows missing or deleted sales receipts missing
- *prevention:* explain and let employees know management is checking the loss prevention awareness report and question employees whose names appear frequently on the report

Product Theft and Prevention Examples

Types, indicators, and possible prevention of internal product thefts are listed below.

Outright Concealed Theft (Hidden On the Person, In Trash, Bags, Purses, and So On)

- *indicators:* product missing but not sold; product found concealed (in the back room, counter areas, and so on); suspicions reported by others
- *prevention:* articles like coats and knapsacks should be held in the "safe" area (an area under management watch, a locked room or counter area, with the caveat posted that management is not responsible for lost or stolen personal belongings); products found concealed should be put away immediately after an incident report is written; management should ask all employees the reason the product was concealed; trash removal should be carried out under management supervision, with a manager unlocking the door, watching as trash is removed, and relocking the door; employees should make purchases only at quitting time, and management should sign off and ring up any purchases by employees; products purchased by employees should be bagged and sealed immediately

Unauthorized Discounts/Markdowns

- *indicators:* markdown percentages are larger than regular sale markdown percentages; unusual markdowns are found on the loss prevention awareness reports

- *prevention:* closely monitor markdown percentages; inform employees of unusual increases and make inquiries of employees when unusual markdowns are discovered; monitor employees who may ring up products frequently for friends, employees of neighboring stores, and so on

Giving Product Away (to Friends, Employees of Neighboring Businesses)

- *indicators:* product missing from inventory but not sold; persons seen leaving the store with product that appears to have not been rung up (no bag or register ticket)
- *prevention:* be aware of what employees are doing at the cash drawer when waiting on friends, employees of neighboring stores, and so on; check register reports periodically after transactions involving employees' friends and known acquaintances

Handling A Dishonest Employee

There may be times when you'll be confronted with a dishonest employee. Each situation is different, but certain requirements and procedures must always be followed. Any employee who suspects another employee is dishonest must report the suspicion to the store management, district manager, regional or district loss prevention manager or other designated source. Examples of situations that develop are listed below, along with the procedure for handling the situation.

- *situation:* an employee is suspected of dishonesty

  procedure: notify your loss prevention manager or district loss prevention manager, who will work with you to resolve the problem; institute prevention techniques that you feel can prevent the suspected loss

- *situation:* an employee or customer reports a dishonest employee

  procedure: obtain as many details as possible from the person who reported the incident--who was involved, when did it happen, where did it happen, how did it happen, and exactly what happened; document all the information received and notify your loss prevention manager or district loss prevention coordinator; work together to resolve this problem immediately; monitor the employee and institute prevention techniques that will prevent further loss

- *situation:* an employee is caught with or is under the influence of drugs or alcohol while at work

  procedure: it's best to confront the employee in private (in a conference room or back room). Once you have received a verbal statement from the employee, document everything in your notes as it was said. The employee should be given the opportunity to present his or her side of the incident. Give the employee a pen and paper and ask him or her to write a statement describing the incident in his or her own words. This statement should include:

    - employee's name, store number, and the date
    - any admissions of theft or dishonesty the individual gave orally

- identification of item taken
- time and method in which it was taken
- why the individual took it
- exactly what occurred (a description of the incident)
- length of time employee has been with the company
- signatures of the employee and of a manager

In every case of employee theft or drug use, a "statement of fact report" must be completed. Notify Loss Prevention before the employee leaves the store. The final disposition of the incident will be the responsibility of the loss prevention manager. Gather all reports obtained in the incident and forward them to your loss prevention manager.

Suspend the employee for theft unless instructed differently by your store, district, or regional loss prevention manager.

Management Techniques for Prevention

All managers have their own styles and use their own techniques in managing their stores. Here are some important techniques that should be actively used in internal loss prevention in your store.

- **Open communication channels.** This technique can be developed by openly discussing losses and their prevention with all employees. Managers asking questions about discrepancies, suspicions, and problems will make employees aware of the concern. This will directly influence the reduction or prevention of losses. Discuss loss prevention at every store meeting.

- **Hiring.** Managers who develop interviewing and screening techniques can hire honest employees who will be willing to follow policy, procedure, and guidelines.

- **Developing.** By developing employees in loss prevention, management will have a trained sales staff and a trained loss prevention staff.

- **Inventory Control.** Many prevention techniques branch out from inventory control. Practicing such techniques as keeping accurate inventories, being aware of stock on hand vis-a-vis stock sold, product organization, ordering, receiving, upstocking, merchandising, and controlling inventory may prevent employees from becoming dishonest.

- **Follow-up/Verification.** Constant follow-up and verification of discrepancies, suspicions, mistakes and reported problems can determine causes of loss and assist in future prevention. At the same time, this will communicate a high level of awareness. Your loss prevention awareness report is one of the best tools you can use.

- **Outside Communication.** To obtain additional information and answers, communicate with your district manager, regional manager, loss prevention manager, and auditing and loss prevention departments.

- **Cash Control.** Monitor discrepancies and patterns to begin identifying causes of cash losses, then use cash control techniques in conjunction with policies and procedures to reduce and eliminate opportunity for loss.

Something as natural as getting to know the employee you work with is a management technique. Try to develop and actively use the techniques listed below every day. Recognizing these qualities in each one of us will help develop your staff and make it more effective.

- set and enforce clear expectations and standards
- keep the workplace well organized and neat
- emphasize good customer service
- have adequate coverage of the customers' needs
- maintain professional attitudes
- establish regular channels for information feedback
- encourage all employees to believe in and follow company policies
- maintain and secure a safe working environment for all employees
- encourage strong belief in and support of loss prevention activities
- follow up on problem indicators
- establish effective loss prevention orientations for all new hires
- get all employees working in employee/management teams
- talk about loss prevention on the job or in store meetings
- double-check all book work
- review register reports on transaction deletions and security violations

Losses Resulting from Errors

In most cases, losses attributable to error can be prevented by identifying the errors and correcting them. In many cases employees can develop controls to reduce or eliminate opportunities for errors. The most important aspect of control is training. Management that trains employees during orientation and checks on their progress will be able to effectively reduce the opportunities for errors.

Cash Losses Resulting from Errors

Listed below are key areas where cash losses can occur and where extra attention should be focused on initial employee training and reinforced during meetings and day-to-day activities.

Focus

Cash Drawers

- drawer operation
- issuing and redeeming documents
- acceptance of checks and charges
- audit procedures
- cash handling and cash drops
- voids
- markdowns

Applications in Rental Situations Like Video Stores

- establishing and following damaged rental procedures
- acceptance, filing and return of deposits
- handling and filing
- entries (especially manual ones)

Opening and Closing

- accuracy in processing beginning and ending bankdrafts
- buying change
- check, charge, and document placement and totaling
- deposit verification

Management Focus

Drawer Audit Procedures

- monitoring reconciliation
- reviewing cash drops from each cash drawer
- store bank and cash drawer access control
- excessive markdown

Closing Paperwork

- correct totaling of all documents
- placing documents in a secure location
- daily closing envelope entry completed properly
- register reports

Bank Deposits

- verifying cash totals to be deposited
- listing checks accurately for deposit
- accurately completing bank deposit slips
- verifying cash counts and document totals with a second employee

Double-checking documents and training store personnel are major factors in controlling, identifying, correcting and reducing losses by human error and paperwork errors.

Product Loss Resulting from Error

Listed below are areas in which product losses occur as a result of error. Always complete an Incident Report on any product loss, from error or otherwise.

Receiving/Shipping

- Carton counts: always note any carton shortages
- Packing slips: be sure to list all discrepancies
- Ticketing: review for correct pricing
- Damage: note on packing slip, receiving memo, and freight bill
- Product received: transfer all product to receiving memo accurately
- Product placed in wrong area

Because small pieces are shipped and received, check all cartons before throwing them away. Also, store any overstock cartons rather than setting them loosely on shelves.

Price Changes

- Price change entries: enter correct quantities and amounts
- Thoroughness: check for product missed (out-of-place) and reordered
- Reticketing after a price change

Store Returns

- Carton count: verify carton accountability on the bill of lading
- Bill of lading and supplement: information must be accurate

Physical Inventory

- Pricing: correct ticketing before inventory begins
- Actual counts: stress importance of counting all product accurately

Defectives

- Filing: keeping and filing all defectives for return credit (never destroy damaged product)
- Ringing up all product
- Ringing correct prices
- Marking down only sale product
- Entering correct reasons for voids

Stock/Fixture Maintenance

- Product that falls behind or in-between fixtures may be mistakenly overlooked during regular and physical inventories

Our Employees...

...are our most important asset, so the first rule that applies to internal or external prevention is employee safety.

Rules for employee safety

- No amount of cash or merchandise is of greater value than your safety
- At no time should an employee risk his or her own safety or the safety of another
- Whenever possible, management should handle any irregular or unusual incident
- Never use physical force
- If a situation should get out of control or appear to be at all dangerous, back away (contact mall security or the police)
- If an incident involving any type of weapon or robbery occurs, it is best to remain calm and cooperate completely.

The well-being of all associates is our primary concern. Contact the store's management or your regional loss prevention office if anyone's safety is ever threatened. Any incident involving safety or accidents (of employee or customer) is to be documented on an incident report and reported immediately.

Night Closing

- All customers must be out of the store and all doors locked prior to removing and counting any cash, checks, or credit card drafts for closing procedures. During day shifts, cash drawers are to be counted and listed in the audit sheet out of customer view
- At no time is anyone (friend or customer) allowed to come into or be in the store after closing
- The closing management must leave the store with at least one employee. No employee (management or otherwise) is to be in the store after closing procedures are complete
- Prior to leaving the store, look outside and insure that there are no suspicious persons in the parking lot. Leave together and go directly to your car. Once in your car, lock the doors and drive out of the lot when other employees are leaving.

CHAPTER FOUR

Indicators and Prevention of External Dishonesty

In this section we will identify types of external losses and procedures that can prevent them from occurring.

Types of External Losses

Review the list below to identify types of external loss.

- Shoplifting
- Boosting
- Credit card fraud
- Counterfeit, altered bills
- Shortchange artists
- Robbery
- Burglary
- Exchange return fraud
- Ticket switching
- Shipping and receiving errors and misrepresentations
- Property or product damage from floods, fires, vandalism, etc.
- Document fraud (forged gift certificates and credit slips, and so on)
- Threats/extortion (bombs, strongarm physical force, and so on)

Identifying Thieves

Shoplifters and boosters will signal that they are about to steal by their actions and characteristic movements and body language. These will warn employees in advance of their intentions. The following are some of the telltale characteristics that theft is likely to occur.

A shopper or shoppers—

- remaining in the store or a particular section of the store for a long time
- wandering aimlessly around the store
- appearing nervous or tense
- carrying an open bag, purse, package, or knapsack
- carrying a large amount of merchandise
- pushing a baby stroller or carrier (with or without a baby)
- wearing extra large baggy clothing or a large coat
- carrying a coat draped over shoulder or arm
- returning to the store two or more times in the same day
- purposely attempting to distract employees (look for possible accomplices)

If you identify likely shoplifters, offering to wait on them or simply keeping a watch on them will most often prevent theft. But action must be implemented immediately to avoid losses. Management must always be told of any suspicious actions.

Customer Service and Loss Prevention

Customer service and observing the store is the first step to preventing loss. Even while renting, selling, or stocking, employees must look up from time to time, thinking, "Are we being ripped off?"

Observing customers' actions, appearance, and so on, is the first step in helping them. Not all customers are alike. Some need a good deal of help, some simply have a question or two, some may be suspicious-looking and warrant added customer service to prevent loss or other problems. Always observe customers before approaching them.

Be aware of "blind" spots or problem areas in your store.

If you feel that a customer is doing something that could lead to theft, notify store management immediately and approach the customer. Make eye contact, smile, and say hello. That's all it takes! You need not begin a long conversation right away.

Greeting a customer (or potential thief) does three things.

- It discourages shoplifters because they have already been seen.
- It lets them know you care about helping them (and about stopping theft).
- It identifies you as the "professional" or "expert."

External Theft Prevention Procedures

- When at a workstation, always watch the sales floor.
- While inventorying merchandise, always face the sales floor or glance around the store often. If an employee's back is to the sales floor, a shoplifter may use the opportunity to steal.

- Always keep merchandise (other than displays) off sales counters. If a customer selects an item, offer to ring it up. Don't let the customer walk around the store with concealable items.
- Beware of shoppers who try to attract your attention away from the sales floor or who drop items over the counter, forcing you to bend down and pick them up.
- Keep track of the number of behind-the-counter items handed to a customer. Make sure all items not selected for purchase are put back.
- Watch for more than usual numbers of items being located in the wrong section, or quantities of items out-of-order in under stock (booster set-up). If a set-up is found, notify management immediately and return the product to its correct section.
- Check risk areas in your store frequently. Thefts usually occur in areas hidden from view, like back corners and spaces behind large displays.
- Keep all stock well organized and evenly distributed. This often discourages shoplifters and boosters and makes it easier to identify a set-up or anything else out of the ordinary.

Confrontations

The company's policy for theft is prosecution, but it's very important that specific legal guidelines be followed before a decision to prosecute is made. If prevention techniques are not possible, it may be necessary to apprehend a shoplifter. Apprehensions can take place only when all the following apply.

The Six Rules for Successful Apprehension of Shoplifters

1. You must have seen the person remove an item from display and know that the item is store merchandise.
2. You must have seen the item being concealed and know where it was concealed.
3. You must have watched the shoplifter at all times after the item was concealed and know that the shoplifter did not remove the item from his person.
4. You must be able to say that the shoplifter made no attempt to pay for the item.
5. Before apprehending the shoplifter, he or she must be outside the store exit without having attempted to pay.
6. If the item is concealed on the shoplifter's person, in his or her clothing, you cannot take it away unless it is offered voluntarily. If the shoplifter denies having taken the item and you are 100 percent sure that it is concealed on his or her person, only then can the police conduct a search of the person. Ask the shoplifter to come back into the store. Note: if you believe the merchandise has been concealed in a bag marked with the store name, you may conduct a search of that bag only.

What to Say and Do

Once you have fulfilled the six above rules, you should--

- Escort the suspect back inside the store
- Call the police

- Complete an Incident Report, Statement of Fact and Apprehension Report. If all of these are fill out completely, the company can recover at least $150 in civil cases.
- Never use physical force to detain or apprehend a suspect. Remain calm and make no threats or promises.
- If an arrest is made, label the merchandise recovered with the suspect's name, the date, and names of employees involved in the incident. Place the shoplifted merchandise in a box and seal it. This should be held in the office or storeroom for evidence (but for no longer than 90 days). It is to be counted in all physical inventories.
- Send the Statement of Fact, Incident Report, Apprehension Report and any other documentation (police report, witness statement, and so on) to your loss prevention manager who will log and file it for later use or reference and restitution.
- Always be as accurate and detailed as possible when documenting incidents. In some cases, an employee may need to testify and documentation will assist in remembering exactly what happened.

Cash Drawer Security

Review the following descriptions of types of theft from cash drawers.

- **Short change artists** first attempt to make small purchases using large bills. When counting back change, they attempt to confuse clerks by asking for more change or different change. The entire process takes no more than 30 to 60 seconds.

If a small purchase is made using a 10, 20, etc., pull the correct amount of change from the drawer, then close and lock the cash drawer and carefully count back the change. When the customer requests change for the bills, explain politely that you can't make change. If he or she persists, call Management.

- **Till tap artists** may work alone or with one or two accomplices. They either open the cash drawer while you are away or when you are distracted. They may even make a small purchase. They generally distract the clerk by:
  - spilling coins over the counter to force the clerk to pick them up
  - asking questions or trying to make the clerk turn and look away
  - knocking over a counter display
  - reaching across the counter into the open cash drawer and pulling out bills while the employee is distracted.

Here are tips on preventing till taps.

- always close the cash drawer immediately after a transaction
- always lock the cash drawer and remove the key if you leave the immediate area
- always keep as few bills as possible in your drawer
- if you feel someone is attempting to distract you, and may be a till tap artist, slow down, and call a co-worker or manager for assistance
- drop large bills (50s and 100s) immediately.

Theft

Theft occurs in several ways. Keep an eye out for these potential tip-offs.

- customers using false ID or stolen credit cards or checks
- returns of reproduced (bootleg) instead of original merchandise (as in video rentals)
- customers falsely stating that merchandise is defective to avoid having to pay for it
- switched labels
- stolen cards
- outright theft off the shelves or within customers' reach
- customers giving false information on credit or membership applications
- customers returning rental merchandise directly to shelves without paying (as in video stores)
- checks without customer's full name, address, and telephone number.

Procedures for Preventing Video Theft at Video Stores

Reproduced Movies

- Visually examine video returns. If the factory label has been peeled off, steamed off or the original is switched with an unlabeled tape, notify store management. The customers will then realize that check-in clerks are aware of altered videos. Incidents have been reported of spools being replaced entirely. This can easily be detected because plastic guards over the screws that hold the cassette together have to be removed in order to remove the spools.

Visually examine videos prior to customers' renting or returning them to determine whether the video rented is a reproduction. This method will increase the chances of not having a reproduced video already in stock.

Stolen Credit Cards with Video Club Membership Stickers

- As more video club members are added, attempted use of stolen credit cards will increase. With the average value of rental videotapes being approximately $200 to $300 in cost and lost income, it is extremely important to visually check the customer's name and driver's license number against the name and number of the card they present (this is company policy). Follow video guidelines to prevent use of stolen cards with membership stickers.

Customer Service

- Good customer service in the video display area will also prevent theft. Keeping the area neat, clean, and well organized will reveal any missing merchandise. All returned videotapes should be placed in the library area immediately and never left on the counter or within reach of customers.

  Any employee who suspects video theft should notify store management immediately.

Robberies

Most robberies occur in late afternoon or at night. Potential robbers may not be easily identified until a robbery actually occurs. Watch for the following.

- suspicious persons lingering around the store, inside or out
- anyone lingering near closing time
- anyone lingering in a car or outside the store around the time deposits are taken to the bank. Call your regional loss prevention manager if this occurs.

Robbery Prevention

Follow these procedures and guides to limit the risk of robbery in your store.

- always keep cash drawer keys on the person of the drawer operator
- never allow cash in drawer to build up
- make drops as frequently as possible, especially after dark
- always keep the safe locked and the safe keys on the person of the manager in charge
- always prepare drops and count them out of customer view
- never call out a cash drop or how much the drop will be
- always put drops directly into the safe; never carry them around or set them down
- don't open the doors for anyone before the store opens or after it closes

- never make a bank deposit at night; take them in the morning before the store opens. Only members of management should make deposits.
- never count out audit drawers or safe change in view of customers; find a secure place where it can be done
- if an employee suspects that someone is watching him or her who may be a robber, that employee should notify the police immediately by dialing 911.
- Consider installing time-delay locks in store safes.

If a Robbery Occurs

Try to remain as calm as possible and try to cooperate with the suspect 100 percent. During a robber, do exactly as the robber says.

- Once you're sure the robber has gone, the store management must immediately telephone the police. Do not pursue the robber
- Close the store and ask all witnesses to remain in the store until the police arrive
- Notify Loss Prevention immediately
- Write down a description of the person in full detail
- Have any and all associates and customers write down what they saw
- Send all documents and an incident report to the Loss Prevention Department

Cooperate fully with police and their investigation. Call your district manager before reopening the store.

Shipment Shortage Prevention

Shipment shortages are the easiest shortages to prevent, by following the receiving instructions. Here are a few reminders to further prevent losses.

- Compare the cartons shipped to the number of cartons listed on the invoice
- Be sure all cartons are sealed on the top and the bottom (check for resealing)
- Examine damaged cartons
- Check the contents of any cartons that are opened or have been damaged before the delivery driver leaves
- Do not allow truck drivers or delivery drivers to leave before the shipment has been checked
- Always note any discrepancies, damage, or pieces missing on the packing slip and receiving memo
- Note product discrepancies found during receiving on the packing slip, receiving memo, and complete an incident report
- Never take the deliverer's word for carton counts or that he or she will deliver missing cartons later

Credit Card/Check Fraud

Thousands of dollars are lost each year in our company as a result of credit card and check fraud. Credit card and check fraud can easily be prevented by simply identifying them when they occur. Here are ways to identify and prevent fraud when customers are using credit cards, personal checks and travelers' checks.

Credit Card Fraud Prevention

Fake or altered credit cards can be identified in a number of ways.

- If the name on the credit card does not match the name on the person's driver's license
- When the signature on the credit card does not match the signature on the draft or the person's driver's license
- Expired credit card date
- Signature erased or altered on back of card
- Embosses raised letters that appear to be altered or flattened out (as with pressing with a hot iron)
- Cards that appear cut, bent, or partially mutilated

Follow these procedures to reduce the use of fraudulent credit cards:

Step 1: Examine the card, the expiration date, the customer's name, and so on. Look for any of the fraud identifiers previously listed

Step 2: Match the name on the credit card against the driver's license

Step 3: Match the signature on the credit card, the charge draft, and the driver's license to be sure that they are the same

Step 4: Examine the driver's license. Compare the photo with the customer's appearance, and the signature on it with the signature on the draft. All must match.

PROCESSING THE CREDIT CARD

5277 0606 0004

1362 06/86

MR. JOHN DOE

120186

PURCHASER SIGN HERE

X

Cardholder acknowledges receipt of goods and/or services in the amount of the Total shown hereon and agrees to perform the obligations set forth in the Cardholder's agreement with the Issuer.

5540401

CURRENCY CONVERSION DATE			RATE	AMOUNT
QUAN.	CLASS	DESCRIPTION	PRICE	AMOUNT
DATE	AUTHORIZATION	MasterCard	SUB TOTAL	
REFERENCE NO.	CLERK/DEPT.	VISA	TAX	
SALES SLIP			TOTAL	

SAFEIPERF® U.S. Pat. 4,403,793

SALES SLIP
BANK PROCESSING COPY

BANK COPY

If the card being used is not the customer's, call management and politely tell the customer the card can't be accepted. Hold the product and void the sale with management present. An incident report should be filled out whenever an attempt is made by a customer to use a stolen or fraudulent credit card. Read and post any security bulletins that contain instructions on non-acceptance or confiscation of credit cards. If a card is called in for verification, follow all instructions after getting the operator's name.

If in doubt about any credit card transaction, call the card in.

Check Fraud Prevention

Fraudulent checks can easily be identified by these characteristics.

- Any personalized check without a preprinted name and address
- A name on a check that does not match the name on the identification of the person trying to use it
- Pen alterations or marks over account numbers across the bottom of a check
- Eraser marks on a check, or what appear to be faded paper, ink smudges or a feathered or bleached stain
- Checks with no customer address preprinted
- Checks with no bank name or bank address
- Checks without bank ID numbers in the upper right corner
- Pre- or post-dated checks, or pre-signed checks
- Checks in which the dollar amount appears to have been altered

To reduce the possible acceptance of fraudulent checks, follow all check acceptance polices and note these procedures:

- Examine the check to make sure it is filled out completely
- Match the customer's name, signature, and picture with the driver's license. Obtain a second piece of identification and repeat the visual match

If a check appears to be fraudulent, altered, or unpersonalized, the management should explain to the customer that it cannot be accepted

Travelers' Check Fraud Prevention

Fraudulent travelers' checks can be identified by the following characteristics:

- A second signature that does not match the original signature
- A pre-signed signature
- A travelers' check good for pounds sterling, pesos, or anything other than U.S. dollars

To reduce the possible acceptance of fraudulent travelers' checks, follow all travelers' check acceptance procedures, including:

Step 1: Examining the check to make sure it is in U.S. dollars

Step 2: Requiring the customer to sign the check in your presence (do not accept a pre-signed check)

Step 3: Matching the signatures and obtaining a piece of identification (driver's license, passport, state ID, and so on). Always stamp travelers' check with your store check stamp and write the ID on the appropriate lines

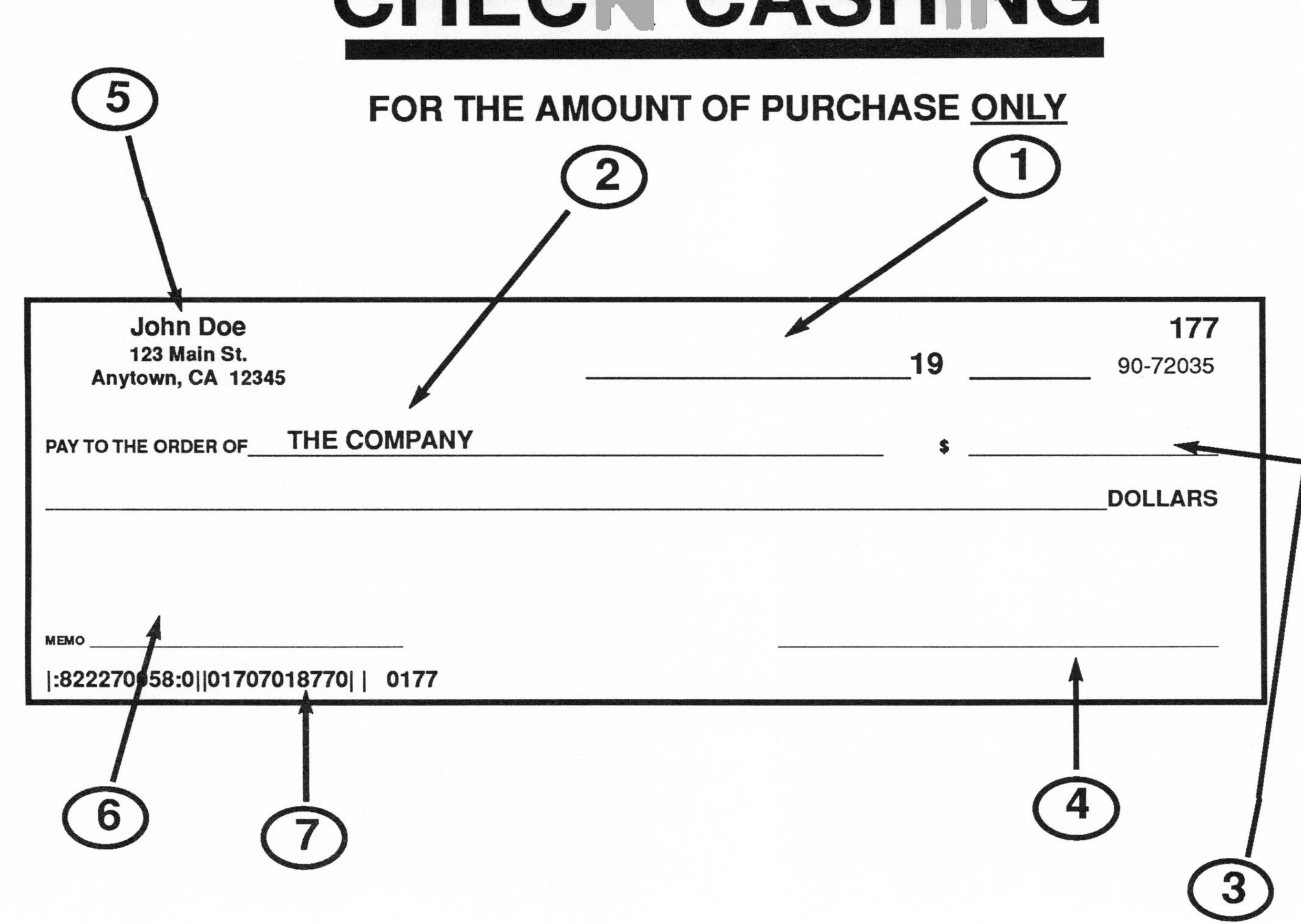
FOR THE AMOUNT OF PURCHASE ONLY
5
2
1
John Doe
123 Main St.
Anytown, CA 12345
177
19
90-72035
PAY TO THE ORDER OF THE COMPANY
$
DOLLARS
MEMO
|:822270558:0||01707018770|| 0177
6
7
4
3

CHECK APPROVAL

PAY TO THE ORDER OF

NATIONAL BANK
YOUR COMPANY NAME

YOUR ACCOUNT NUMBER

DL# ______________ (1)
BIRTHDATE ______________ (1)
TYPE OF CD. ❑ AE ❑ MC ❑ V (2)
CR. CD. # ______________ (2)
EXPIRE DATE ______________ (2)
CHECK APPROVAL # ______________ (3)
CKS INITIALS ______________ (4)
VRA # (IF RENTAL) ______________

MWA (5)

WE DO NOT CASH MONEY ORDERS

Counterfeit Bill Prevention

An increase in the number of counterfeit bills in circulation requires that we focus attention on preventing these bills from being used at our store. Most counterfeit denominations are twenties, fifties, and 100 dollar bills. They are usually found by the bank after we have sent in our deposits.

Identifying Counterfeit Bills

The following are ways to identify counterfeit bills and persons attempting to use them. It's important to remember that passing a counterfeit bill is a federal offense. Counterfeit bills are identified in a number of ways. Watch for the following signals.

- Bills that seem irregular in appearance (very dark, sections faded, torn or ragged edges; see examples)
- Persons attempting to use large bills for small purchases (inserts for 45 rmp records, 45 records themselves, batteries, and so on)
- Bills that feel very much like regular paper (actual treasury bills are made of cotton fiber)
- Ink on a bill that appears cracked., faded, smeared, or discolored
- Bills with features that appear dull, undefined, or with irregularities or unevenness in letters or numbers
- Absence of blue or red fibers meshed in a bill
- Overall poor quality appearance
- Corners of 20s pasted on one dollar bills
- A president's face that does not correspond to the denomination of the bill

Prevention of Counterfeit Acceptance

To prevent acceptance of counterfeit bills, review the following procedure and information:

- When accepting a 20, 50, or 100 dollar bill, look for an unusually small purchase being made. Ask for smaller bills.
- Visually examine the bill. If it appears irregular in any way, notify management.
- If a customer asks to change a 20, 50, or 100 dollar bill, politely tell him or her you cannot give change for large bills. If they insist, allow management to handle the situation and visually check the bill.

Procedure for accepting large bills

- If a 50 or 100 dollar bill is tendered, management is to be notified immediately (company policy). The bill should be checked carefully by management. If the bill looks counterfeit, do not accept it. Notify Loss Prevention.
- If a counterfeit bill is in the store cash, fill out an incident report and include the bill in the regular bank deposit.
- Always "Drop" large bills immediately.

Counterfeiting

"Counterfeiting is an offense never committed by accident, nor by ignorance, nor in the heat of passion, nor in the extreme of poverty. It is a crime expertly designed by one who possesses technical skill and lays out substantial sums for equipment."

Robert H. Jackson (1892-1954) Associate Justice, U.S. Supreme Court

Counterfeiting of money is one of the oldest crimes in history. It was a serious problem in the early days of our country when banks issued their own currency. By the time of the War Between the States, it was estimated that one-third of all currency in circulation was counterfeit.

At that time, there were approximately 1,600 State Banks designing and printing their own notes. Each note carried a different design, making it difficult to distinguish the 4,000 varieties of counterfeits from the 7,000 varieties of genuine notes.

It was hoped the adoption of a national currency in 1863 would solve the counterfeiting problem. However, the national currency was soon counterfeited so extensively it became necessary for the Government to take enforcement measures. Therefore, on July 5, 1865, the United States Secret Service was established to suppress counterfeiting.

On a genuine bill the saw-tooth points of the Treasury seal are clear, distinct and sharp. The counterfeit Treasury seal may have uneven, blunt or broken saw-tooth points.

The fine lines in the border of a genuine bill are clear and unbroken. On the counterfeit the lines in the outer margin and scroll work may be blurred and indistinct.

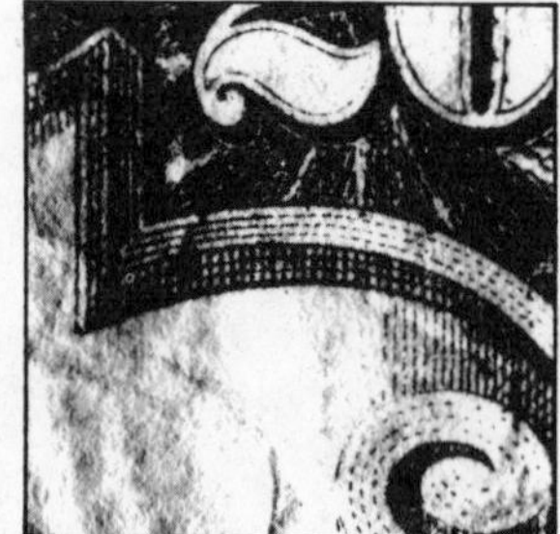

Genuine serial numbers have a distinctive style and are evenly spaced. They are printed in the same ink color as the Treasury seal. On a counterfeit the serial numbers may differ in color or shade of ink from the Treasury seal. The numbers may not be uniformly spaced or aligned.

Genuine paper money looks good because it is printed from engraved steel plates by experts, using equipment and paper designed for that purpose.

Counterfeit paper currency looks bad because it is usually produced by a photo-offset process with equipment and paper designed for other purposes.

Genuine paper contains no watermarks. It has tiny red and blue fibers imbedded throughout. These fibers are not embedded in the counterfeit, although they are sometimes simulated by surface printing.

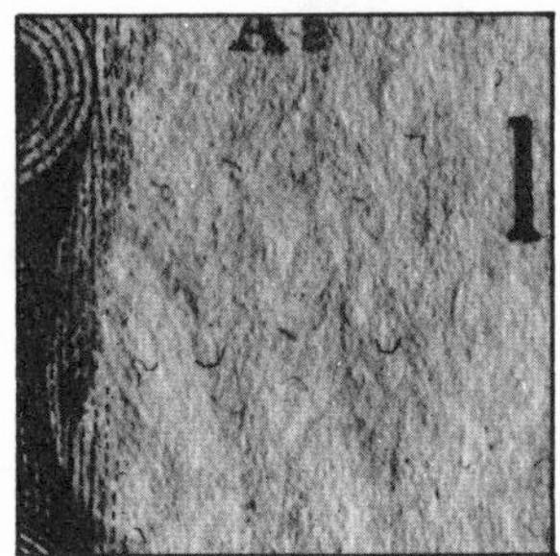

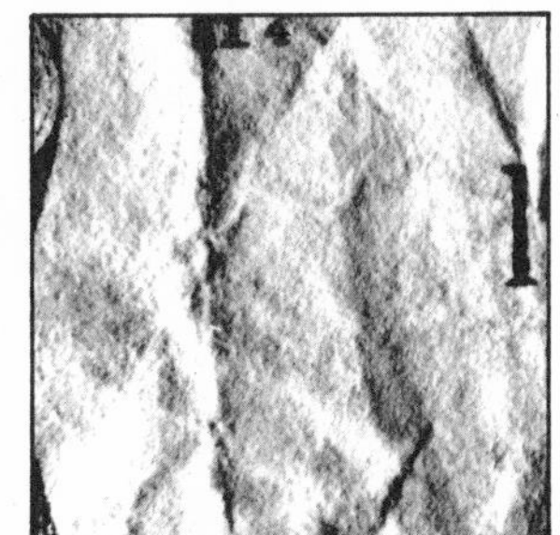

The genuine portrait appears lifelike and stands out distinctly from the fine screen-like background. The counterfeit portrait is usually lifeless and flat. Details merge into the background which is often too dark or mottled.

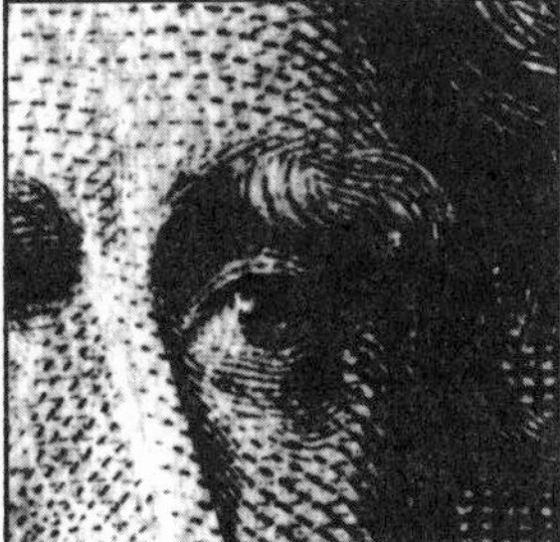

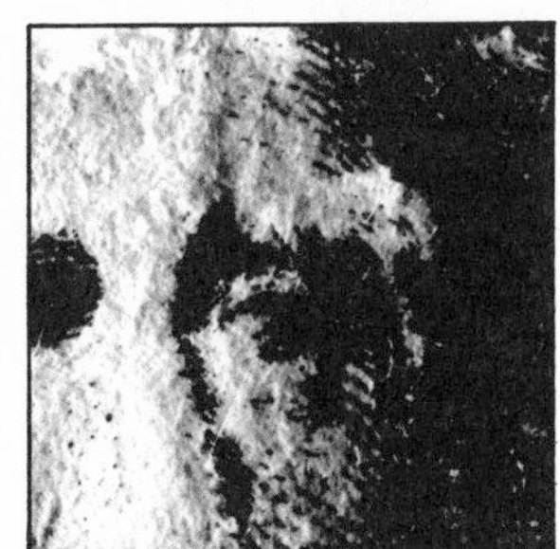

Portraits and Back Designs on Paper Currency

$1
George Washington
Great Seal of the United States

$2
Thomas Jefferson
Declaration of Independence

$5
Abraham Lincoln
Lincoln Memorial

$10
Alexander Hamilton
U. S. Treasury Building

$20
Andrew Jackson
White House

$50
Ulysses S. Grant
U. S. Capitol

$100
Benjamin Franklin
Independence Hall

LOSS PREVENTION TOOLS

F.A.S. Systems or alarms, card access

Catching shoplifters is not the best way to reduce shoplifting losses. Keeping them out of the store is even better.

Electronic Article Surveillance

Stores use two types of systems, magnetic and microwave, for electronic article surveillance. These systems are not apprehension devices, they they are designed to prevent shoplifting in stores.

Testing and Maintenance

To insure that your systems are operational, you must test them daily before opening the store and log the activations on a System Activity log.

Before calling, please check the immediate area of the system for metal objects or signs, loose tags, or any items listed in the Sensormatic Operation Manual. All calls and service must be reported on your activation logs. If your system is not repaired within 72 hours, please notify the Loss Prevention Department for assistance.

Tagging Product Priorities

All product must be tagged according to the priority listed below:

First:

Second:

Third:

Fourth:

Fifth: All designated product

For detailed instructions on tagging application, see the Sensormatic Operation Manual.

Closed-Circuit Television (CCTV)

Most stores are equipped with closed-circuit television systems. These systems are designed to prevent loss by observing "hard-to-see" areas of the store. If this system malfunctions in any way, contact the maintenance department.

Locks and Keys

Stores are equipped with the system locks and keys. The cores are interchangeable, and the keys cannot be duplicated by regular locksmiths. If a key is lost, immediately contact your Loss Prevention Manager to change the core and issue new keys.

Customer Flow Barricades

Customer flow barricades are designed to regulate the flow of customers to workstations that are staffed. Use of these barricades will reduce the possibility of individuals leaving the area with concealed product.

Alarm System

The alarm system is the key factor in your store's protection from the time the doors are locked until they are reopened the next morning. It is imperative that set time guidelines for entry and exit be followed to avoid false alarms and costs of police responses. Always notify your district or regional office of new management appointments, or terminations, to avoid misunderstandings by the alarm company. Always be sure to alarm is set and on before leaving the store.

____

Write entry time in pencil

____

Write exit time in pencil

____

Alarm company phone number

If early entry or late closing is necessary, you must contact your district manager for approval and notification to the alarm company.

WARNING: You are never to reenter the store after the alarm has been set.

If management is contacted at night regarding an alarm break or for not setting the alarm, management is required to respond immediately.

If personnel or phone number changes are made within management, it is the manager's responsibility to supply the district manager the new names and phone numbers. The district manager will then update the alarm company in writing.

Other Tools

Stores may also be equipped with iron gates, U-locks, time-delay lock safes, and so on. The proper use of these tools will help to prevent external theft and losses in the store.

Loss Prevention Structure — Where to Get Help

Your immediate contacts in the Loss Prevention Department are your regional loss prevention manager and district loss prevention coordinator. They can be contacted for any loss prevention emergencies, reports of dishonesty or theft, questions, clarifications, or training.

CHAPTER FIVE

Commonly Used Drugs in the Workplace

Drugs most commonly used at the workplace are heroin, marijuana, cocaine, amphetamines, barbiturates, LSD, DNT, STP, PCP, crack and ICE.

The use, selling, being under the influence of or possession of any alcohol, intoxicating or illegal drug or substance is considered illegal and a violation of company policy.

Knowledge of any employee in violation of this policy is to be documented and reported to Store Management or Corporate Loss Prevention immediately. The company may use drug testing for pre-employment, promotional or investigative purposes.

American industry must awaken and recognize the growing problem of theft and drug abuse in the workplace. Consider these news items:

- At the Social Security Administration in Baltimore, 18 persons were arrested in March 1985 and charged with possession of cocaine, marijuana, and amphetamines.
- At Armatron in Melrose, Mass., nine persons were arrested in June 1985 and charged with possession of cocaine, marijuana, amphetamines, and LSD.

- At the Seabrook, N.H., nuclear power plant construction site, 14 persons were arrested in January 1985 and charged with possession of marijuana and amphetamines.

- Four Phase Systems, Division of Motorola Corp., Cupertino, CA, 3 were arrested in July, 1980 and charged with sales of cocaine, marijuana and amphetamines.

- At Compugraphic Corp. in North Reading, Mass, 13 persons were arrested in March 1985 and charged with possession of marijuana, LSD, mescaline, and amphetamines.

Examples of lost time

The examples are merely the tip of the iceberg—the cases investigated with resulting arrests. No one knows the full magnitude of the problem, but it's sure to get worse as those who grew up using drugs join the work force.

The drug abuser requires different treatment than the alcoholic. Although both exhibit some of the same symptoms, drug abusers obtains their supplies from illegal sources and frequently may be involved in illegal activities to support their habits.

Let's consider some of the problems to be expected because of drug abuse by employees.

- Lost time resulting from absences or inability to function on the job
- Reduced liability
- Diminished performance
- Higher-than-average susceptibility to injury with possible liability on the part of the employer. If injury occurs on the job, injured employees may submit claims that injuries were caused by job conditions rather than drug abuse
- Higher-than-average susceptibility to illness caused by weakened physical condition, leading to lost time
- Loss of security clearance, either for the individual or for the company's facility
- Escalating financial needs to meet growing drug demands, which can lead to theft, fraud, and embezzlement
- Vulnerability to coercion and blackmail
- Potential emergence of organized groups involved in abuse and sale of drugs and in related criminal activities; drug abuse is a social activity
- Possible introduction of outside criminal elements providing the drugs and/or market for equipment and information stolen from the company
- Higher insurance rates for the company resulting from medical, thefts, fraud, and embezzlement claims.

What Can Be Done?

Among the first steps to be taken in controlling employee drug abuse is the *establishment of an official company policy toward abuse and abusers.* From this, comprehensive programs can be developed. The programs fall into two categories: preventive and remedial.

Screening job applicants to identify abusers can reduce the number of potential problem employees. Background investigations provide the most effective screening technique, but may not be cost- or time-effective for many organizations. Instead, interviewers can be trained to eliminate the more obvious problem applicants For sensitive positions, more thorough screening standards can be compiled.

Letting job applicants know clearly what the company's policies and procedures are (including rehabilitation and counseling programs and possible dismissal from employment) can discourage drug abusers form accepting positions with the company, and later deter some potential abusers.

Identifying The Problem

- The remark, "We live in a drug-oriented society," has been made repeatedly. Our citizens have been conditioned to expect rapid relief from any discomfort, unease, or other form of real or imagined psychophysical distress. Increasing numbers of people seek chemical solutions for shyness, boredom, and tensions. They turn to drugs to create positive mood states.
- While the use and abuse of drugs may provide the desired effect for the individual, the side effects and consequences of drug abuse

have a major impact on the workplace. A recent study by the White House Office on Drug Policy revealed that businesses lose $10.3 billion annually from employee problems related to drug use.

- Drug abuse contributes to lower production, difficult relationships with co-workers, inadequate attention and concentration, memory lapses, tardiness, and absenteeism.
- Employers and supervisors no longer can avoid the drug issue by claiming it does not effect job performance. An "as long as the job gets done" attitude only ignores the problem. Co-workers share also in the responsibility of identifying a drug problem in their workplace, out of interest for their own safety, if not out of human compassion.
- It is important that each person, worker or supervisor, be cognizant of the problem of drug abuse. The following information will assist in recognizing the popular substances of abuse, the physical symptoms produced, and the danger presented to the abuser. By being able to recognize the symptoms associated with drug abuse, you will be in an enlightened position to refer the individual to the proper assistance unit.

Symptoms

- Mood swings; periods of high energy followed by periods of depression
- Sleepy appearance
- Irritability; nervousness or anxiety for no apparent reason

- Smoking; sharp increase within a short period of time
- Loss of appetite
- Unusual amount of time spent in locked bathroom or isolated locations
- Bloodstains on shirtsleeves
- Marks on arms or legs caused by injections
- Wearing of long-sleeved shirts, even in warm weather
- Glassy stare (fish eyes)
- Dilated pupils
- Presence of pill bottles, capsules, needles, eye-dropper, syringe, burnt spoons or bottle caps, glassine envelopes
- Unexplained disappearance of radios, cameras, watches, office equipment, and the like
- Watery eyes, running nose
- Dreamy or blank expression; drunk appearance
- Lack of coordination, confusion
- Excessive itching
- Craving for sweets
- Slurred speech
- Aggressive behavior, giggling, rapid speech
- Severe hallucinations; cold hands and feet; vomiting.

Commonly Used Drugs (Controlled Substances)

Different drugs have different effects on users.

Heroin

- Is derived from morphine.
- Is generally a white powder, but may vary in color form yellow to brown, depending on the country of origin. Heroin is known by many names by users and pushers: horse, H, scat, junk, snow, stuff, Harry, big H, joy powder, dope, and other names.

Morphine

- Is known by such names as white stuff, Miss Emma, dreamer, M (tablets).

Codeine

- Is known as Schoolboy (tablet and liquid).
- *Physical symptoms:* Stupor/drowsiness; needle marks on body, generally on arms; watery eyes; loss of appetite; blood stains on shirtsleeves; running nose.
- *Look For:* Needle or hypodermic syringe; cotton; tourniquet; string; ropes; belt; burnt bottle caps; spoons; glassine envelopes.
- *Dangers:* Death from overdose; mental deterioration; destruction of brain and liver; hepatitis; embolisms and related problems associated with use of non-sterile needles.
- *Cough medicine-can contain both codeine and opium.*
- *Physical Symptoms:* Drunk appearance; lack of coordination; confusion; excessive itching.

- *Look For:* Empty or partially filled bottles of cough medicine.
- *Dangers:* Causes addiction.

Marijuana

- Is found generally in the form of a hand-rolled thin cigarette, and is known as pot, grass, tea, gage, reefers, smoke. It also is packaged as loose, leafy particles in manila envelopes or plastic bags.
- *Physical Symptoms:* Sleepiness; wandering mind; enlarged eye pupils; lack of coordination; craving for sweets; increased appetite.
- *Look For:* Strong odor of burnt leaves; discarded small seeds; cigarette papers; discolored fingers.
- *Dangers:* Inducement to take stronger narcotics; may create a psychological dependence on marijuana; is believed to cause physical side effects worse than tobacco.

Cocaine

- Is a white crystalline powder normally inhaled through the nose, but it also can be injected hypodermically. It is known as coke, snow, blow, flake, happy dust, C, or crack.
- *Physical Symptoms:* Periods of high energy followed by depression, *paranoia.*
- *Look For:* Small vials; thin foil packets, doubled-foiled on ends; hollow tubes; small spoons; plastic vial or bottle used to store crack (looks like rock candy).

- *Dangers:* Death from overdose; hallucinations; methamphetamine sometimes cause temporary psychosis.

Barbiturates

- Are pills or capsules of varying colors, known as barbs, blue devils, candy, yellow jackets, phennies, peanuts, blue heavens, goofballs, or downs.
- *Physical symptoms:* Drowsiness; stupor; dullness; slurred speech; drunken appearance; vomiting.
- *Look For:* Pills or capsules of varying colors.
- *Dangers:* Death from overdose, or causes addiction, convulsions, and death as a result of withdrawal.

LSD, DNT, and STP

- Are liquids known as acid, sugar, big D, cubes, trips, or businessman's high.
- *Physical Symptoms:* Severe hallucinations; feeling of detachment; incoherent speech; cold hands and feet; vomiting; laughing and crying.
- *Look For:* Cube sugar with discoloration in center; strong body odor; small tube of liquid; blotter paper with discoloration.
- *Dangers:* Extremely dangerous, can produce suicidal tendencies, unpredictable behavior; chronic exposure cause s brain damage; LSD causes chromosomal breakdown.

Crack pipe (glass)

Crack or hashish
placed on screen
and lit

Screen
(changed often)

Mouthpiece

Liquid coolant

Methamphetamine pipe (glass)

Crystal meth placed
in bowl

Mouthpiece

Hole

Milky white residue forms
on the inner bowl following
frequent use

Bottom of bowl heated until meth turns to
gas. It is then inhaled.

PCP

- Comes in the form of liquid tablets and powder, and can be dusted on mint, parsley, or marijuana leaves. It is known as dust, peace, pill, and hog.
- *Look For:* Odor of ether or acetone.
- *Dangers:* Unprovoked violence; psychotic behavior. The side effects listed here obviously indicate that drugs are extremely dangerous to the mental and physical health of the abuser In many instances the drug abuser also is a menace to others. For example, and addict must secure money to purchase drugs and will steal any item of value to get funds. An individual high on LSD may cause damage to plant equipment or injury to co-workers.

In order to confirm suspicions, a number of diagnostic test are available to the industrial physician or other qualified person trained to collect specimens. Application of these tests on an industry-wide basis is relatively new, and knowledge regarding their availability is not as common as it might be.

Treatment and counseling are available to drug abusers in private and public programs, and assistance is available to companies in organizing treatment programs.

Generally, local and State Departments of Health sponsors such assistance.

Review of Drugs and More:

Depressants

In excessive amounts depressants induce a state of intoxication remarkable like that of alcohol.

Depressants have a high potential of abuse associated with both physical and psychological dependence.

Taken as prescribed by a physician, depressants may be beneficial for the relief of anxiety, irritability, and tension, and for the symptomatic treatment of insomnia. In excessive amounts, however, they produce a state of intoxication that is remarkably similar to that of alcohol.

As in the case of alcohol, these effects may vary not only from person to person but from time to time in the same individual. Low doses produce mild sedation. Higher doses, insofar as they relieve anxiety or stress, may produce mood depression and apathy. In marked contrast to the effects of narcotics, however, intoxicating doses invariably result in impaired judgment, slurred speech and loss of motor coordination, resulting in high incidence of highway accidents. Recurrent users incur risks of long-term involvement with depressants.

Tolerance to the intoxicating effects develops rapidly, leading to a progressive narrowing of the margin of safety between an intoxicating and a lethal dose. The person who is unaware of the dangers of increasing dependence will often increase the daily dose up to 10 or 20 times the recommended therapeutic level. The source of supply may be no farther than the family medicine cabinet. Depressants are also frequently obtained by theft, illegal prescription, or by purchase on the illicit market.

Members of the drug subculture often resort to using depressants as self-medication to soothe jangled nerves brought on by the use of stimulants, to quell the anxiety of "flashbacks" resulting from prior use of hallucinogens, or to ease their withdrawal from heroin. The dangers, it should be stressed, are compounded when depressants are used in combination with alcohol or other drugs. Chronic intoxication, though it affects every age group, is most common in middle age. The problem often remains unrecognized until the user exhibits recurrent confusion or an obvious inability to function. Depressants also serve as a means of suicide, a pattern particularly common among women.

As will be shown, the depressants vary with respect to their potential for overdose. Moderate depressant poisoning closely resembles alcoholic inebriation. The symptoms of severe depressant poisoning are coma, a cold clammy skin, a weak and rapid pulse, and a slow or rapid but shallow respiration. Death will follow if the reduced respiration and low blood pressure are not counteracted by proper medical treatment.

The abrupt cessation or reduction of high-dose depressant intake may result in a characteristic withdrawal syndrome, which should be recognized as a medical emergency more serious than that caused by any other drug of abuse. An apparent improvement in the patient's condition may be the initial result of detoxification. Within 24 hours, however, minor withdrawal symptoms manifest themselves, among them anxiety and agitation, loss of appetite, nausea and vomiting, increased heart rate and excessive sweating, tremulousness and abdominal cramps.

The symptoms usually peak during the second or third day of abstinence from the short-acting barbiturates or meprobamate; they may not be reached until the seventh or eighth day of abstinence from the long-acting barbiturates or benzodiazephiens. It is during the peak period that the major withdrawal symptoms usually occur. The patient may experience convulsions indistinguishable form those occurring in grand mal epilepsy. More than half of those who experience convulsions will go on to develop delirium, often resulting in a psychotic state identical to the delirium tremors associated with alcohol withdrawal. Detoxification and treatment must, therefore, be carried out under close medical supervision. While treatment techniques vary to some extent, they share common objectives: stabilization of the drug-dependent state to allay withdrawal symptoms followed by gradual withdrawal to prevent their recurrence.

Among the depressants that give rise to the general conditions described are chloral hydrate, a broad array of barbiturates, glutethimide, metaqualone, meprobamate, and the benzodiazepines.

Chloral Hydrate

The oldest of the hypnotic (sleep-inducing) drugs, chloral hydrate was first synthesized in 1862 and soon supplanted alcohol, opium, and cannabis preparations for inducing sedation and sleep. Its popularity declined after the introduction of the barbiturates, but chloral hydrate is still widely used. It has a penetrating, slightly acrid odor, and a bitter caustic taste. Its depressant effects, as well as resulting tolerance and dependence, are comparable to those of alcohol, and withdrawal symptoms resemble delirium tremors. Chloral hydrate is a liquid, marketed in the form of syrup and soft gelatin capsules. Cases of poisoning have occurred from mixing chloral hydrate with alcoholic drinks. Chloral hydrate is not a street drug of choice . Its main misuse is by older adults.

Barbiturates

Among the drugs most frequently prescribed to induce sedation and sleep by both physicians and veterinarians are the barbiturates. About 2,500 derivatives of barbituric acid have been synthesized, but of these only about 15 remain in medical use. Small therapeutic doses tend to calm nervous conditions, and larger doses cause sleep 20 to 60 minutes after oral administration. As in the case of alcohol, some individuals may experience a sense of excitement before sedation takes effect. If dosage is increased, however, the effects of the barbiturates may progress through successive stages of sedation, sleep, and coma to death from respiratory arrest and cardiovascular complications.

Barbiturates are classified as ultrashort-, short intermediate-, and long-acting. The ultrashort-short acting barbiturates produce anesthesia within one minute after intravenous administration. The rapid onset and brief duration of action make them undesirable for purposes of abuse. Those in current medical use are hesobabital (Evipal), methohexital (Brevital), thiamylal (Surital), and thiopental (Pentothal).

Among the short-acting and intermediate-acting barbiturates are pentobarbital (Nembutal), secobarbital (Seconal), and amobarbital (Amytal), three of the drugs in the depressant category most sought-after by abusers. The group also includes butabarbital (Butisol) butalbital (Lotusate), allobarbital (Dial), aprobarbital (Alurate), and vinbarbital (Delvinal). After oral administration, the onset time of action is from 15 to 40 minutes and duration of action is up to six hours. Physicians prescribe short-acting barbiturates to induce sedation or sleep. Veterinarians use pentobarbital for anesthesia and euthanasia.

Long-acting barbiturates, which include barbital (Veronal), phyenobarbital (Luminal), mephobarbital or methylphenobarbital (Medbaral), and methorbital (Gemonil) have onset times of up to one hour and durations of action up to 16 hours. They are used medicinally as sedatives, hypnotics, and anticonvulsants. Their slow onset of action discourages their use for episodic intoxication, and they are not ordinarily distributed on the the illicit market except when sold as something else. It should be emphasized, however, that all barbiturates result in a buildup of tolerance, and dependence on them is widespread.

Gluthethimide

When gluthethimide (Doriden) was introduced in 1954, it was said to be a safe barbiturate substitute without an addiction potential. But experience has shown glutethimide to be another CNS depressant, having no particular advantage over the barbiturates and several important disadvantages. The sedative effects of glutethimide begin about 30 minutes after oral administration and last for four to eight hours. Glutethamide is marketed as Dorident in 125-, 250-, and 500-mg tablets. Because the effects of this drug are of long duration, it is exceptionally difficult to reserve overdoses, which often result in death.

Methaqualone

Methaqualone is a synthetic sedative chemically unrelated to the barbiturates, glutethimide, or chloral hydrate. It has been widely abused because it was once mistakenly thought to be nonaddictive and effective as an aphrodisiac. Actually, methaqualone has caused many cases of serious poisoning. It is administered orally. Large doses cause coma, which may be accompanied by thrashing movements or convulsions. Continued heavy use of large doses leads to tolerance and dependence Methaqualone has been marketed in the United States under various brand names various brand names such as Quaalude, Parest, Optimil, Somnafac, and Sopor. Counterfeit Quaalude tablets, which do not necessarily contain methaqualone, are prevalent on the U.S. illicit market, similar in appearance to the 300-mg tablet formerly distributed by Rorer. Mandrax is a European brand name for methaqualone in combination with antihistamine. Mecloqualone, a chemical similar to methaqualone in all significant respects, is not legally sold in the United States.

Meprobamate

Meprobamate, first synthesized in 1950, introduced the era of "minor" tranquilizers. In the United States today, more than 200 tons of meprobamate are distributed annually under its generic name as well as under brand names such as Miltown, Equanil, Kesso-Bamate, and SK-Bamate. Meprobamate is prescribed primarily for the relief of anxiety, tension, and associated muscle spasms. Its onset and duration of action are like those of the intermediate-acting barbiturates; it differs from them in that it is a muscle relaxant, does not produce sleep at therapeutic does, and is relatively less toxic. Excessive use, however, can result in psychological and physical dependence. Mebutamate (Dormate), is a drug similar to meprobamate in its chemical makeup and effects.

Benzodiazepines

The benzodiazepine family of depressants relieve anxiety, tension, and muscle spasms, produce sedation, and prevent convulsions. These substances are marketed as mild or minor tranquilizers, sedatives, hypnotics or anticonvulsants. Their margin of safety is great than that of other depressants. Eight members of the group are currently marketed in the United States. They are chlordiazepoxide (Librium), chonazepam (Clonopin), clorazepate (Tranxene, Azene), diazepam (Vallum), flurazepam (Dalmane), lorazepamm (Ativan), oxazepam (Serax), and parzepam (Verstran). Librium and Valium are among the drugs most widely prescribed in this country. These drugs have a relatively slow onset but long duration of action. Prolonged use of excessive doses may result in physical and psychological dependence. Withdrawal symptoms develop approximately one week to 10 days after continual high doses are abruptly discontinued. The delay in the appearance of the abstinence syndrome is a result of the slow elimination of the drug from the body. When these drugs are used to obtain a "high," they are usually taken in conjunction with another drug such as alcohol or marijuana.

Stimulants

Of all abused drugs, stimulants are the most powerfully reinforcing. They can lead to increasingly compulsive behavior.

The two most prevalent stimulants are nicotine in tobacco products and caffeine, the active ingredient in coffee, tea, and some bottled beverages that are sold in every supermarket. When used to moderation, these stimulants tend to relieve fatigue and increase alertness They are an accepted part of our culture.

There are, however, more potent stimulates which, because of their dependence-producing potential, are under the regulatory control of the Controlled Substances Act. These controlled stimulants are available on prescription for medical purposes; they are also clandestinely manufactured in vast quantities for distribution on the illicit market.

Users tend to rely on stimulants to feel stronger, more decisive, and self-possessed. Because of the cumulative effects of the drugs, chronic users often follow a pattern of taking "uppers" in the morning and "downers" such as alcohol or sleeping pills at night. Such chemical manipulation interferes with normal body processes and can lead to mental and physical illness.

Young people who resort to stimulants for their euphoric effects consume large doses sporadically, over weekends or at night, often going on to experiment with other drugs of abuse. The consumption of stimulants may result in a temporary sense of exhilaration, super-abundant energy, hyperactivity, extended wakefulness and a loss of appetite; it may also induce irritability, anxiety, and apprehension. These effects are greatly intensified with administration by intravenous injection, which may produce a sudden sensation known as a "flash" or "rush." The protracted use of stimulants is followed, however, by a period of depression known as "crashing" that is invariably described as unpleasant. Since the depression can be easily counteracted by a further injection of stimulant, this abuse pattern becomes increasingly difficult to break. Heavy users may inject themselves every few hours, a process sometimes continued to the point of delirium, psychosis, or physical exhaustion.

Tolerance develops rapidly to both the euphoric and appetite-suppressant effects. Doses large enough to overcome the insensitivity that develops may cause various mental aberrations, the early signs of which include repetitive grinding of the teeth, touching and picking face and extremities, performing the same task over and over, a preoccupation with one's own thought processes, suspiciousness, and sense of being watched. Paranoia with auditory and visual accountancy characterizes the toxic syndrome resulting from continued high doses. Dizziness, tremor, agitation, hostility, panic, headache, flushed skin, chest pain with palpitations, excessive sweating, vomiting, and abdominal cramps are among the symptoms of a sublethal overdose. In the absence of medical intervention, high fever, convulsions, and cardiovascular collapse may precede the onset of death. It should be added that physical exertion increases the hazards of stimulant use since accidental death is caused in part by the drugs' effects on the cardiovascular and body temperature regulating system. Fatalities under conditions of extreme exertion have been reported among athletes who have taken stimulants in moderate amounts.

If withdrawn from stimulants, chronic high-dose users exhibit profound depression, apathy, fatigue, and disturbed sleep for up to 20 hours a day. The immediate withdrawal syndrome may also be a lingering impairment of perception and thought processes. Anxiety, an incapacitating tenseness, and suicidal tendencies may persist for weeks or months. Many experts now interpret these symptoms as indicating that stimulant drugs are capable of producing physical dependence. Whether the withdrawal syndrome is physical or psychological in origin is in this instance academic, since the stimulants are recognized as among the most potent agents of reward and reinforcement that underlie the problem of dependence.

Cocaine

The most potent stimulant of natural origin, cocaine is extracted from the leaves of the cocoa plant (rythroxylon coa), which has been cultivated in the Andean highlands of South America since prehistoric times. The leaves of the plant are chewed in the region for refreshment and relief from fatigue, much as North Americans once chewed tobacco.

Pure cocaine, the principal psychoactive ingredient, was first isolated in the 1880's. It was used as an anesthetic in eye surgery for which no previously known drug had been suitable; it became particularly useful in surgery of the nose and throat because of its ability to constrict blood vessels and thus limit bleeding. Although many of its therapeutic applications are now obsolete, the legal use of cocaine in the United States has in recent years been increased by the introduction of a morphine-cocaine elixir designed to relieve the suffering associated with terminal illness. In England, where this mixture was developed at the Brompton Chest Hospital, the use of cocaine in treatment of the terminally ill was largely abandoned after it was determined that it contributed to disquieting hallucinations and nightmares.

Illicit cocaine is distributed as a white crystalline powder, often adulterated to about half its volume by a variety of other ingredients, the most common of which are sugars such as actose, inositol, mannitol, and local anesthetics such as lidocaine. Since the cost of illicit cocaine is high, there is a tendency to adulterate the product at each level of distribution. The drug is most commonly administered by being "snorted" through the nasal passages. Symptoms of repeated use in this manner may resemble the congested nose of a common cold. Less commonly, for heightened effect, the drug is injected directly into the bloodstream. Unlike such drugs as LSD and heroin, cocaine is popularly accepted as a recreational drug, facilitating social interaction. It is erroneously reputed to be relatively safe from undesirable side effects Because of the intensity of its pleasurable effects, cocaine has the potential for extraordinary psychic dependency, which is all the more deceptive in view of its reputation as the recreational drug of choice.

Recurrent users may resort to larger doses at shorter intervals until their lives are largely committed to their habituation. Anxiety, restlessness, and extreme irritability may indicate the onset of a toxic psychosis similar to paranoid schizophrenia. Others are persecuted by the fear of being watched and followed. Excessive doses of cocaine may cause seizures and death from respiratory failure.

Crack (cocaine)

The most popular drug today is 90 percent pure cocaine, minimum 2/3 cocaine, 1/3 baking powder or lactose, the cocaine in Item I above is only 30 to 40 percent, mixed with the same percentages, and is usually snorted through the nose and is in powder form. Crack cocaine is usually in a rock form and is made by mixing with water until it forms a paste and is then allowed to dry. The only difference is the main ingredient is 90 percent pure and is heated. When this is done it forms a liquid and is shot directly into the bloodstream. Example: 2/10 of an ounce of regular cocaine in Item I above usually takes approximately 20 minutes, compared with crack cocaine which, using the same dosage takes approximately two seconds to run through the bloodstream. The result is a quicker high but it doesn't last as long.

Approximate Costs:

1 Gram	=	$80.00 to $100.00
1 Oz.	=	$500.00 to $800.00
1 Pound	=	$6,000.00 to $9,000.00
1 Kilo	=	$12,000.00 to $17,000.00

The costs above vary from time to time depending on the demand. For example, the price in Chicago or New York would be more than if you bought the drug at point of entry.

Amphetamines, ice (methamphetamines)

Amphetamine, dextroamphetamine, and methamphetamine are so similar in the effects they induce that they can be differentiated from one another only by laboratory analysis. Amphetamine was first used clinically in the mid-1930's to treat narcolepsy, a rare disorder resulting in an uncontrollable desire for sleep. After the introduction of amphetamines into medical practice, the number of conditions for which they were prescribed multiplied as did the quantities made available. They were sold without prescription for a time in inhalers and other over-the-counter preparations. Abuse of the inhalers became popular among teenagers and prisoners. Housewives, students, and truck drivers were among those who used amphetamines orally in excessive amounts, and "speed freaks," who injected them, won notoriety in the drug culture for their bizarre and often violent behavior. Whereas a prescribed dose is between 2.5 and 15 mg per day, those on a "speed" binge have been known to inject as much as 1,000 mg every two or three hours. Recognition of the deleterious effects of these drugs and their limited therapeutic value has led to a marked reduction in their use by the medical profession. The medical use of amphetamines is now limited to narcolepsy, hyperkinetic behavioral disorders in children, and certain cases of obesity<197>as a short-term adjunct to a restricted diet for patients refractory to other forms of therapy. Their illicit use closely parallels that of cocaine in the range of its short-term and long-term effects. Despite broad recognition of the risks, clandestine laboratories produce vast quantities of amphetamines, particularly methamphetamine for distribution on the illicit market.

"Crystal meth" ("ice age" in Hawaii)

GENERAL HISTORY

Methamphetamine is a form of amphetamine, a stimulant. Stimulants are compounds which affect the central nervous system by accelerating its activities.

Stimulants are either natural, such as Epinephrine and Norepinephrine, or synthetic such as Amphetamine and Phenmetrazine. The first natural stimulant was Epinephrine (adrenaline) and the effects were first described in 1899. The first synthetic stimulant of any significance was prepared in 1919 by a Japanese chemist and was later identified as Methamphetamine.

Amphetamine was first synthesized in the 19th Century but was not widely used medically until the 1930's when it was introduced as a treatment for narcolepsy and as an ingredient in decongestant inhalers. Its properties as a stimulant caused the use of amphetamine to grow steadily in the 40's through the 70's, when it was used for a number of problems including depression, lethargy, and fatigue. According to sources, Methamphetamine was used by soldiers in the Korean army during World War Two. This enabled them to continue fighting for long periods of time with very limited rest and food consumption. These drugs reached great popularity in the 60's and 70's when they were used in diet pills.

Today, the legal use of Amphetamine is limited to the treatment of narcolepsy (a rare disorder resulting in an uncontrollable desire for sleep), peritonitic behavioral disorders in children, and certain cases of obesity. Crystal Meth or "ice" first appeared in Hawaii during 1985 but was not recognized as a problem until 1987. During that time, local Filipino gang members were the principal distributors for "ice."

WHAT IS METHAMPHETAMINE?

Methamphetamine is the most pericardia of the amphetamine group and is available in pharmaceutical tablets under the trade name "Desoxyn" (refer to PDR, edition 40, 1986, Abbot laboratories, photo-page 403, description-page 513). It is listed as a Schedule II drug under Chapter 329 of the Uniform Controlled Substances Act.

Methamphetamine has often been called the poor man's cocaine and has traditionally been the drug of choice of outlaw motorcycle gangs. Commonly called "meth," "crystal" (powder form or "crank," long-time street term for "speed," usually referring to the pill variety). In Honolulu, "crystal" or "ice" is used to refer to the rock Methamphetamine and "crank" is the term used for the powder form.

HOW IS IT RECOGNIZED?

On the mainland, Methamphetamine is normally found as a white powder. In Hawaii, it is in the form of a translucent crystal similar in appearance to "rock candy" or "Hawaiian salt." "Ice" found in Hawaii is a very pure form of Methamphetamine (98 to 100 percent pure).

HOW IS IT USED?

Methamphetamine can be injected, inhaled, smoked, or taken orally. In the Honolulu area, the most common method has been to smoke the drug using a glass pipe. See attached illustration of a Meth pipe. It is said that a person can obtain approximately 10 to 15 hits from 1 gram of "ice."

HONOLULU STREET INFORMATION

Information gathered in the Honolulu area indicates that several forms of crystal meth are being used. Most prevalent is the translucent or clear rock crystal. This form of meth is said to be water-based and burns quickly, leaving a milky white residue on the inside of the bowl. Reports also show that a yellowish crystal meth is also available. This form of meth is said to be oil-based. This form of yellow meth is also said to burn slower and last longer, leaving behind a brownish or black residue in the pipe.

Crystal meth, "ice," is presently being sold in the Honolulu area in quantities ranging from .10 gram to an ounce. Price for a .10 gram is $50.00, with the cost of an ounce going for approximately $7,000.

EFFECTS AND HAZARDS

Users feel an intense wave of physical and psychological exhilaration. The effects of the drug may last from four to 14 hours, depending on the dosage. Although entering the bloodstream rapidly, large doses may be excreted into the urine, unchanged, up to 72 hours after ingestion. Methamphetamine use tends to keep the user awake and alert and provides temporary mood elevation, and continued use causes the body to deplete its stored energy. This lack of sleep/rest prevents the replenishment of these reserves. Insomnia is usually followed by sleeping for long periods.

PHYSICAL EFFECTS

The drug tends to overtax the body and causes the body to literally burn itself up. Vitamin and mineral deficiencies are common because of inadequate nutrition as the user keeps pushing beyond what the body can tolerate and may lead to a rapid and noticeable loss of weight. There is lowered resistance to disease and prolonged use will cause damage to organs, particularly to the lungs, liver, and kidneys.

PSYCHOLOGICAL EFFECTS

Continued use of methamphetamine can cause a heavy degree of psychological dependence on the drug which leads to a psychotic state, insomnia, anxiety, depression, and fatigue. Toxic psychosis similar to paranoid schizophrenia can result from heavy short- or long-term use, as well as delusional states. Prolonged use can also produce a heavy degree of psychological tolerance, and users find they have to use heavier dosages.

DANGERS

Withdrawal from methamphetamine does not involve physical discomfort but can involve depression and fatigue. Depression can reach critical proportions, since life seems boring and unpleasant. Progressive toxic effects of amphetamine abuse may include restlessness, tremors, talkativeness, irritability, insomnia, anxiety, delirium, panic states, paranoid ideation, palpitation, cardiac arrhythmias, hypertension, circulatory collapse, dry mouth, nausea, vomiting, abdominal cramps, convulsions, coma and *death.*

Other dangers include rapid deterioration of physical and psychological health, since methamphetamine erases feelings of periods of time and creates the same sort of stress to the body that any long period of exertion creates. However, the user does not let his body recuperate and permanent damage or death is the result.

As of August, 1989, 25 percent of newborn infants tested in Hawaii showed traces of crystal meth in their systems. Queens Hospital was averaging approximately a half dozen meth overdoses a day, compared to one a day the previous year.

PARAPHERNALIA

Common carriers for meth are opaque glass vials, paper bindles, or, more commonly in Honolulu, clear heat-sealed cellophane packets. Common paraphernalia includes syringes for the user who injects his drugs or glass smoking pipes (Bongs).

There is a difference between a pipe used for cocaine and that used by the meth smoker. The basic difference is in the construction of the pipe. Refer to Figure A for an illustration of the differences in the construction of these pipes.

The cocaine pipe is made of two sections, one to hold the cocaine and the other section to hold a liquid coolant. The sections are separated by a screen or similar object. Cocaine smokers will ignite the cocaine in the top half of the glass pipe. The fumes are then inhaled, first through the coolant chamber and then into the mouth.

The "meth" or "ice" pipe has only one section where the methamphetamine is placed and heated. There are no screens and no coolants in the meth pipe. The pipes used for smoking meth usually have a hole on the top of the bowl leading to the main chamber and may have a vent hole on the stem between the chamber, where the crystal is placed, and the mouthpiece.

The "ice" is first placed into the chamber and heated with a lighter or other heat source until it turns to a gas. The opening in the chamber and venthole are sealed, usually with a finger, while the crystal is being heated. Once the crystal has turned to gas, it is inhaled by the user. A telltale sign of a meth user is the presence of burn marks on the finger(s) used to seal the hole in the main chamber.

HOW ICE IS MADE

The "meth" or "ice" is placed in a bowl or container, mixed with warm water until a paste forms, then is put into the freezer of the refrigerator and allowed to harden. When it is in the freezer it forms into a crystal rock, just like rock candy.

Phenmetrazine (Preludin) and Methylphenidate (Ritalin)

The medical indications, patterns of abuse, and adverse effects of phenmetrazine (Preludin) and methylphenidate (Ritalin) compare closely with those of the other stimulants. Phenmetrazine is medically used only as an appetite suppressant and methylphendidate mainly for the treatment of hyperkinetic behavior disorders in children. They have been subject to abuse in countries where freely available, as they are here in localities where medical practitioners write prescriptions on demand. While the abuse of phenmetrazine involves both oral and intravenous use, most of that associated with methylphenidate results from injection after the drug in tablet form is dissolved in water. Complications arising from such use are common, since the tablets contain insoluble materials which upon injection block small blood vessels and cause serious damage, especially in the lungs and retina of the eye.

Anorectic drugs

In recent years, a number of drugs have been manufactured and marketed to replace amphetamines as appetite suppressants. These so-called anorectic drugs include benzphetamine (Didrex), chlorphentermine (Pre-Sate, etc.) chlortermine (Vornail), dietthylpropion (Tenuate, Tepanil, etc.), fenfluramine (Pomdimin), maxindol (Sanorex), phendimetrazine (Plegine, Bacarate, Melfiat, Statobex, Tanor ex, etc.), phentermine (lonamin, Apidex-P, etc.). They produce many of the effects of the amphetamines but are generally less potent. Abuse patterns of some of them have not yet been established, but all are controlled because of the similarity of their effects to those of the amphetamines. Fenfluramine differs somewhat from the others in that at low dozes it produces sedation.

Hallucinogens

Natural and synthetic substances that distort the perception of reality.

Hallucinogenic drugs, both natural and synthetic, are substances that distort the perception of objective reality. They induce a state of excitation of the central nervous system, manifested by alterations of mood, usually euphoric, but sometimes severely depressive. Under the influence of hallucinogens, the pupils dilate, the body temperature and blood pressure rise. The senses of direction, distance, and time become disoriented. A user may speak of “seeing” sounds and “hearing” colors. If taken in a large enough dose, the drugs produce delusions and visual hallucinations. Occasionally, depersonalization and depression are so severe that suicide is possible, but the most common danger is impaired judgment, leading to rash decisions and accidents. Persons in hallucinogenic states should therefore be closely supervised, and upset as little as possible, to keep them from harming themselves and others. Acute anxiety, restlessness, and sleeplessness are common until the drugs wear off.

Long after hallucinogens are eliminated from the body, users may experience "flashbacks"—fragmentary recurrences of psychedelic effects—such as the intensification of a perceived color, the apparent motion of a fixed object, or the mistaking of one object for another. Recurrent use produces tolerance, which tends to encourage resorting to greater amounts. Although no evidence of physical dependence is detectable when the drugs are withdrawn, recurrent use tends to produce psychic dependence, varying according to the drug, the dose, and the individual user. It should be stressed that the hallucinogens are unpredictable in their effects each time they are used.

The abuse of hallucinogens in the United States reached a peak of popularity in the late 1960's and a subsequent decline was attributed to broader awareness of their hazardous effects. Their abuse, however, re-emerged in the late 1970's.

Peyote and mescaline

The primary active ingredient of the peyote cactus is the hallucinogen mescaline. It is derived from the fleshy parts or buttons of this plant, which has been employed by Indians in Northern Mexico from the earliest recorded time as a part of traditional religious rites. The Native American Church, which uses peyote in religious ceremonies, has been exempted from certain provisions of the Controlled Substances Act. Peyote, or mescal buttons, and mescaline should not be confused with mescal, the colorless Mexican liquor distilled from the leaves of maguey plants.

Usually ground into a powder, Peyote is taken orally. Mescaline can also be produced synthetically. A dose of 350 to 500 mg of mescaline produces illusions and hallucinations lasting from five to 12 hours.

DOM, DOB, MDA, and MMDA

Many chemical variations of mescaline and amphetamine have been synthesized in the laboratory, certain of which at various times have won acceptance in the drug culture. DOM (4-methyl-2. 5-dimethoxamphetamine), synthesized in 1963, was introduced in 1967 into the Haight-Ashbury drug scene in San Francisco. At first named STP after a motor oil additive, the acronym was quickly reinterpreted to stand for "Serenity, Tranquility, and Peace." A host of related chemicals are illicitly manufactured, including DOB (4-bromo-2 5-dimethoxyamphetamine), and MMDA (3-methoxy-4, 5-methylenedioxyamphetamine). These drugs differ from one another in their speed of onset, duration of action, potency, and capacity to modify mood with or without producing hallucinations. They are usually taken orally, sometimes "snorted," and rarely injected intravenously. Because they are produced in clandestine laboratories, they are seldom pure, and the dose in a tablet, in a capsule, or on a square of impregnated paper may be expected to vary considerably. The names of these drugs are sometimes used to misrepresent other chemicals.

Psilocybin and psilocyn

Like the peyote cactus, Psilcybe mushrooms have been used for centuries in traditional Indian rites. When they are eaten, these "sacred" or magic mushrooms affect mood and perception in a manner similar to mescaline and LSD. Their active ingredients, psilocybin and psilocyn, are chemically related to LSD. They can now be made synthetically, but much of what is sold under these names on the illicit market consists of other chemical compounds.

LSD (LSD-25, lysergide)

LSD is an abbreviation of the German expression for lysergic acid diethylmide. It is produced from lysergic acid, a substance derived from the ergot fungus which grows on rye or from lysergic acid amide, a chemical found in morning glory seeds. It was first synthesized in 1938. Its psychotomimetic effects were discovered in 1943 when a chemist accidentally took some LSD. As he began to experience the effects now known as a "trip," he was aware of vertigo and an intensification of light; closing his eyes, he saw a stream of fantastic images of extraordinary vividness accompanied by a kaleidoscopic play of colors. This condition lasted for about two hours.

Because of the extremely high potency of LSD, its structural relationship to a chemical which is present in the brain, and its similarity in effects to certain aspects of psychosis, LSD was used as a tool of research to study the mechanism of mental illness. It was later adopted by the drug culture. Although its popularity declined after the 1960's, there are indications that its illicit use is once again increasing.

LSD is usually sold in the form of tablets, thin squares of gelatin ("window panes") or impregnated paper ("blotter acid"). The average effective oral dose is from 30 to 50 micrograms, but the amount per dosage unit varies greatly. The effects of higher doses persist for 10 to 12 hours. Tolerance develops rapidly.

Phencyclidine

According to a consensus of drug treatment professionals, phencyclidine now poses greater risks to the user than any other drug of abuse.

Phencyclidine was investigated in the 1950's as a human anesthetic, but because of side effects of confusion and deuterium its development for human use was discontinued. It became commercially available for use in veterinary medicine in the 1960's under the trade name Sernylan. In 1978, however, the manufacturer stopped production. Most, if not all, phencyclidine on the U.S. illicit market is produced in clandestine laboratories.

More commonly known as PCP, it is sold under at least 50 other names that reflect the range of its bizarre and volatile effects, including angel dust, crystal, supergrass, killer weed, embalming fluid, and rocket fuel; it is also frequently misrepresented as mescaline, LSD, or THC. In its pure form a white crystalline powder that readily dissolves in water, most PCP now contains contaminants resulting from its makeshift manufacture that cause the color to range from tan to brown and the consistency from a powder to a gummy mass. Although sold in tablets and capsules as well as in powder and liquid form, it is most commonly applied to a leafy material, such as parsley, mint, oregano or marijuana, and smoked.

The drug is as variable in its effects as it is in appearance. A moderate amount often produces in the user a sense of detachment, distance, and estrangement from his surroundings. Numbness, slurred or blocked speech, and a loss of coordination may be accompanied by a sense of strength and invulnerability. A blank stare, rapid and involuntary eye movements, and a n exaggerated gait are among the more common observable effects. Auditory hallucinations, image distortion as in a fun-house mirror, and severe mood disorders may also occur, producing in some acute anxiety and a feeling of impending doom, in others paranoia and violent hostility. PCP is unique among popular drugs of abuse in its power to produce psychoses indistinguishable from schizophrenia. Although such extreme psychic reactions are usually associated with repeated use of the drug, they have been known to occur in some cases after only one dose and to last, or recur intermittently, long after the drug has left the body.

Modification of the manufacturing process may further yield chemically related analogs, capable of producing, as far as is known, similar psychic effects. Three of these analogs have so far been encountered on the U.S illicit market, where they have been sold as PCP. In view of the severe behavioral toxicity of phencyclidine and its analogs, the Congress in November, 1978, passed legislation imposing penalties for the manufacture of these chemicals, or possession with intent to distribute them, more severe than for any other non-narcotic violation under the Controlled Substances Act. Legislation was also passed which makes it mandatory to report all sales of the common precursor chemical piperidine, its salts, and acyl derivatives to the Drug Enforcement Administration.

Cannabis

According to a recent survey, 43 million Americans have tried marijuana and 16 million used it in the month before the survey.

Cannabis sativa L., the hemp plant, grows wild throughout most of the tropic and temperate regions of the world. It is a single species. This plant has long been cultivated for the tough fiber of the stem, the seed used in feed mixtures, and oil as an ingredient of paint, as well as for the biologically active substances, most highly concentrated in the leaves and resinous flowering tops.

The plant material has been used as a drug for centuries. In 1839 it entered the annals of western medicine with the publication of an article surveying its therapeutic potential, including possible uses as an analgesic and anticonvulsant agent. it was alleged to be effective in treating a wide range of physical and mental ailments during the remainder of the 19th century. With an introduction of many new synthetic drugs in the 20th century, interest in it as a medication waned. The controls imposed with the passage of the Marijuana Tax Act of 1937 further curtailed its use in treatment, and by 1941 it had been deleted from the U.S Pharmacopoeia and the National Formulary, the official compendia of drugs. But advances continued to be made in the chemistry of cannabis. Among the many cannabinolidc acids are cannabigerol, cannabichromene, and several isomers of tetrahydrocannibinol, one of which is believed responsible for most of its characteristic psychoactive effects. This is delta-9-tetra-hydrocannabinol (THC), one of 61 cannabinoids, which are unique chemicals found only in cannabis.

Cannabis products are usually smoked in the form of loosely rolled cigarettes ("joints"). They may be used alone or in combination with other substances. They may also be administered orally, but are reported to be about three times more potent when smoked. The effects are felt within minutes, reach their peak in 10 to 30 minutes, and may linger for two or three hours. A condensed description of these effects is apt to be inadequate or even misleading, so much depends upon the experience and expectations of the individual as well as the activity of the drug itself. Low doses tend to induce restlessness and an increasing sense of well-being, followed by a dreamy state of relaxation, and frequently hunger, especially a craving for sweets. Changes of sensory perception—a more vivid sense of sight, smell touch, taste, and hearing—may be accompanied by subtle alterations in thought formation and expression. Stronger doses intensify these reactions. The individual may experience shifting sensory imagery, rapidly fluctuating emotions, and a flight of fragmentary thoughts with disturbed associations; an altered sense of self-identity; impaired memory, and dulling of attention despite an illusion of heightened insight. This state of intoxification may not be noticeable to an observer. High doses may result in image distortions, a loss of personal identity, fantasies and hallucinations, and very high doses in a toxic psychosis.

During the past 10 years there has been a resurgence in the scientific study of cannabis, one goal of which has been to develop therapeutic agents which, if used as directed in medical treatment, will not produce harmful side effects. While THC can now be synthesized in the laboratory, it is a liquid insoluble in water, and it decomposes on exposure to air and light, so that it is difficult to prepare stable dosage units. Two of the most active areas of research are for the control of nausea and vomiting caused by chemotherapeutic agents used in the treatment of cancer and for decreasing intraocular pressure in the treatment of glaucoma. None of the synthetic cannabinoids have so far been detected in the drug traffic.

Three types of drugs that come from cannabis are currently distributed on the U.S. illicit market.

MARIJUANA

The term marijuana is used in this country to refer to the cannabis plant and to any part of extract of it that produces somatic or psychic changes in man. A tobacco-like substance produced by drying the leaves and flowering tops of the plant, marijuana varies significantly in its potency, depending on the source and selectivity of plant materials used. Most wild U.S. cannabis is considered inferior because of a low concentration of THC, usually less than 0.5 percent. Jamaican, Colombian, and Mexican varieties range between 0.5 and 4 percent. The most selective product is reputed to be sinsemilla (Spanish: sin semilla: without seed), prepared from the unpollenated female cannabis plant, samples of which have been found to contain up to 6 percent THC; Southeast Asian "Thai sticks," consisting of marijuana buds bound onto short sections of bamboo, are also encountered infrequently on the U.S. illicit market.

HASHISH

The Middle East is the main source of hashish. It consists of the drug-rich resinous secretions of the cannabis plant, which are collected, dried, and then compressed into a variety of forms, such as balls, cakes, or cookie-like sheets. Hashish in the United States varies in potency as in appearance, ranging in the THC content from trace amounts up to 10 percent. The average is reported to be 1.8 percent.

HASHISH OIL

The name comes form the drug culture and is a misnomer in suggesting any resemblance to hashish other than its objective of further concentration. Hashish oil is produced by a process of repeated extraction of cannabis plant materials to yield a dark viscous liquid, current samples of which average about 20 percent THC. In terms of psychoactive effect, a drop or two of this liquid on a cigarette is equal to a single "joint" of marijuana.

Inhalants

Amyl and butyl nitrite and nitrous oxide (laughing gas) have not had as much exposure as most of the other illicit drugs. Because of their potential toxicity, we have included the following information

AMYLNITRITE

Over 100 years ago a chemical was introduced to aid patients with the heart condition angina pectoria, or heart spasms, which causes feelings of suffocation and fear. This painful condition was relieved by the use of amylnitrite. Some asthma attacks have also been relieved by the chemical.

In the late 1960's, the Food and Drug Administration became aware that many people were abusing amylnitrite. In 1969, it was changed from an over-the-counter drug to a prescription-only drug because of abuse.

A representative for Burroughs Wellcome, one of the manufacturers of amylnitrite, states that sales continued to rise even after the 1969 restrictions were placed on the chemical. It seems the demand on the street is still strong.

Amylnitrite produces a drop in blood pressure; an expansion, or dilation, of the arteries, especially around the brain; an increase in heart rate, and pressure in the eyeball. The dilation of arteries may produce a flushing sensation. A feeling of lightheadedness, and relaxation of the muscles in the arteries, may occur.

Amylnitrite comes in mesh/cloth-covered glass capsules called ampules. These contain .2 or .03 milliters of clear yellowish liquid. They are broken open and vapors, described as sweet or fruity, are inhaled.

When broken, the ampules make a snapping or popping sound, thus their nickname "poppers" or "snappers." Other nicknames are used, such as "whiffenpoppers," pearls, "amys," or "popsies." They are sold legally as Aspirols or Vaporal.

Over the years, people have found other uses for "poppers." Since the 1930's amylnitrite has had a reputation, mainly around male homosexuals, for prolonging the sensations of sexual climax. Usually, the vapors are inhaled shortly before orgasm.

Medical evidence shows the arteries near the brain expand; oxygen flow to the inner brain decreases; and blood pressure drops. These can distort one's sense of time which can be interpreted as prolonging orgasm. There is no indication that amylnitrite is of benefit in problems of orgasm, nor is it useful in treatment of sexual problems.

Nitrite leaves the bloodstream rapidly, even before the blood pressure returns to normal. Some 60 to 70 percent disappears in the body, partly through oxidation, where a substance combines with oxygen. The fate of the remainder is not known. A small amount is reported to be normally present in the blood, saliva, and sweat.

Orally, amylnitrite is largely destroyed in the stomach and intestines. The liver breaks down the rest. Little reaches the body in an active form.

Amylnitrite injected into veins resulted in few deaths to experimental animals in one study. The inhalation of the vapors by animals, in the same study, resulted in a rapid return to normal with no permanent side effects. The animals suffered vomiting, nausea, and dizziness, as did humans who inhaled nitrite fumes.

Amylnitrite is very volatile, even at low temperatures, and inflammable. It is unstable and decomposes in the presence of air and light.

Side Effects:

- Nausea, vomiting, dizziness and a throbbing headache are side effects of nitrites. They appear to increase when nitrites are combined with alcohol, cocaine, or amphetamines. Symptoms usually last a short time.
- Continued use may cause liver and kidney damage. Amyl liquid in the eye may corrode the cornea, the clear, transparent

outer layer of the eyeball. Use of amylnitrite should be avoided by anemic persons (those who have too few red cells in the blood). It may be harmful to pregnant women and to people with recent head injury, high blood pressure, or a history of cerebral hemorrhaging.

- Despite some of the scare stories, amylnitrite doesn't cause glaucoma (an eye disease). However, it can affect persons who have glaucoma already, because of the increase in inner eyeball pressure.
- Tolerance to nitrites is possible. If one doesn't use them for a couple of weeks, one's tolerance level will return to normal.

Suggested treatment

- If someone has passed out after inhaling nitrites, exposure must be discontinued immediately. Keep the person lying down. If he wakes, encourage him to rest and avoid physical exertion for a while. If the person stops breathing, administer mouth-to-mouth resuscitation. Don't keep the person too warm because nitrites increase blood vessel expansion, vasodilatation. This can be dangerous.

BUTYL NITRITE

Often when one drug has been legally removed from the street market, another one soon takes its place. Thus, the use of butyl nitrite began. It was not presented as a new product for medical use. By advertising it as a "room odorizer" or "liquid incense," the restrictions and controls on amyl nitrite were avoided.

Butyl nitrite, similar in effect to amyl nitrite but with minor differences in chemical structure, is a clear, yellowish liquid. It is available in bars, head shops, record shops, steam baths, porno shops, movie arcades, and through the mail. Although usually sold in small bottles, one company dispenses it in ampules similar to amyl nitrite "poppers."

Across the United States and Canada, butyl nitrite is available under a variety of names: "Jac-aroma," "Mac-Blaster," "Locker Room," "Black-Jac," "Rush," "Bullet," "Crypt," "Heart On," and "Aroma of Man." The most common comparisons of the odor are to "rotten apples" or "raunchy sweat socks."

The side effects of butyl nitrite and treatment for overdose are the same as for amyl nitrite.

The "rush," or physical sensation felt after inhalation of the vapors may last less than one minute, and seldom more than two minutes. At this point, the user usually becomes dizzy and can pass out. A user should be sure that there are no nearby hard or sharp objects on which to fall. "Nose dives" into a hard dance floor can be painful.

Beware of spilling the liquid on your clothing. If a person passes out, the continued inhalation of the fumes can be hazardous.

Although many people claim the use of nitrites is just a passing fad, the chemicals seem to have developed loyal fans in the street market.

An interesting development in the use of amyl/butyl nitrite is that its use seems to be changing from mainly sexual to a more casual "everyday" one. More people are inhaling the nitrites throughout the day. Because the effects are brief, they can be sniffed a dozen or more times in an hour.

Reports from users of butyl nitrite vary greatly as to the pleasant or unpleasant side effects of the chemical. Some users remain faithful only to the "original" chemical, amyl nitrite, and claim that there is no comparison to the cheaper butyl nitrite high; others claim to find no difference between the two.

Curiously no pleasant effects are described by those who take amyl nitrite medicinally. They complain of the odor, pressure in the eyes, or pounding headaches. Recent studies also show that organic nitrites, such as butyl and amyl, can be changed within the body to powerful cancer-causing agents called carcinogens. This can be a serious long-term effect.

Because of the increased abuse of nitrites among young people, eye doctors may be called upon to examine young patients who complain of eye pain and intense headaches. The doctor, therefore, must be alert to the possibility of nitrite abuse.

NITROUS OXIDE

Nitrous oxide, (N_2O) or laughing gas, was discovered by an Englishman named Joseph Priestly. The discovery was made in the 1770's during the experiments in which oxygen was also discovered. In 1779, the gas was inhaled by Humphrey Davey. The high excited him and he told his friends about it.

Davey was joined in the N_2O fan club by such notables as poets Samuel Taylor Coleridge and Robert Southey, China manufacturer Josiah Wedgwood, and Peter Mark Roget, who developed Roget's Thesaurus.

They felt the mood elevation caused by N_2O was much preferable to that of alcohol. Sir Humphrey also noted that N_2O relieved a person's concern about pain, but everyone seemed too involved with the high to investigate the possibility of a useful purpose for the gas.

After 45 years, Horace Wells investigated N_2O's pain-killing potential. Unfortunately, as he was demonstrating his painless dentistry in 1845, at Massachusetts General Hospital, the patient woke up and screamed in pain, somewhat dampening the effectiveness of Wells' suggestion. Despite this little setback, by 1868 N_2O was accepted as an effective painkiller.

N_2O, a colorless gas with a sweet taste and odor, is a compound of nitrogen and oxygen. Its effects are analgesia, euphoria, giddiness, pounding or ringing in the head, altered perceptions, and a dreamy or fantasizing state sometimes referred to as hallucinatory. The gas only takes the patients' mind off the pain by relieving his anxiety. It is not considered sufficient for major surgical procedures without additional anesthesia. It is still used frequently for minor surgery, especially dental surgery.

In surgery, using a nose mask insures that the mouth is kept open to prevent over-medication. This is very important when using N_2O. Without an outside source of oxygen, the body can suffer form oxygen deprivation, which is lack of oxygen to the brain and other organs. This can be avoided either by mixing the oxygen directly into the N_2O or by getting enough air.

Never inhale N_2O while in a car with all the windows rolled up, or in a small enclosed space, such as a closet, without air circulation! The side effects of this include nausea, vomiting, disorientation, and possibly death.

As far as the recreational use goes, it is generally agreed that tanks of N_2O are the cleanest source of laughing gas. Never inhale directly from the tank itself, because the gas can freeze the throat or lips. It can also direct too much air pressure into the lungs.

A common method of N_2O inhalation is the use of empty whipped cream containers with only the propellant (N_2O) left. A recent study of individuals who used this method found that the abusers exhibited numbness of the hands and feet. They also showed a tendency to stagger. Scientists have found that N_2O and up to 26 other compounds are released through these containers.

Researchers don't know what the effects, if any, of many of these other compounds are, but at least three are toxic to the nervous system. Probably the most well-known of these poisons is toluene, one of the harmful ingredients in some glues and lacquer thinners. They also found that the contaminants come from the rubber seal of the whipped cream containers. So, as is the case with so many other chemicals, how the substance is used can make more difference than the chemical itself.

Sniffing

This section is primarily for employers. It's for those whose employer's sniff. And it's for those who don't. It's also for adults fearful of the growing sniffing problem in their stores. We want to dull the edge of fear that many feel about drug abuse generally and sniffing in particular.

At last count, there are 23 chemicals implicated in sniffing abuse. Because thousands of chemicals flood the market each year, the number undoubtedly fluctuates. Cleaning fluids, lighter fluids, paints, paint thinners, shoe polish, spot removers, and hundreds of other products found in the home, school, and workplace are candidates for sniffing abuse. Touene, a widely used chemical, is the one most preferred by sniffers. But they'll choose anything as long as it gets them stoned, is cheap, and is readily available.

Why people sniff

Young people like sniffing because it gets them stoned more quickly than eating or drinking drugs. That's why sniffing is popular and such a problem to control. Sniffing produces changes in the body and it bypasses important processes. Because it's quick and effective, it's popular

Inhaled substances enter the body through the lungs and respiratory tract. Both have large surface areas. chemicals penetrating the cells are absorbed very rapidly and their effects are immediate. This kind of absorption bypasses the body's usual and safer way of breaking chemicals down and sending them through the body.

The usual way is through the stomach and intestines, known as the gastrointestinal system. When substances are eaten or drunk, the gastrointestinal system breaks them down and sends them through the liver.

The liver is the human sewage treatment plant; it removes poisons and sends them to be passed from the body. The whole process takes time. So when the important absorption function of the gastrointestinal system and the detoxification function of the liver are bypassed by sniffing, the chemicals go much more quickly to the brain, where the effects are immediate.

This is the ultimate purpose of all drug use: Make quick change in the brain so changes in perception of the world and oneself happen. As we've pointed out, sniffing makes those changes more quickly than eating or drinking.

What these chemicals do to the body.

Inhalants are central nervous system depressants. They slow down the functions of the brain and spinal chord. In this, they are like alcohol, another brain depressant.

Initial effects of sniffing are relaxation, giddiness, and lessening of inhibition. A sniffer's drunk is similar in many ways to a drinker's drunk. In frequent or high doses, numbing of the senses, hallucinations, and occasionally unconsciousness occurs. The major danger of use is the user's impairment while high; injury comes from bad judgment and lack of coordination.

There's also concern about sniffers' deaths. Usually, death comes form unconsciousness while still exposed to the vapors. Deaths have been reported where sniffers passout with bags still over their heads. The fumes are continuously inhaled and lead to respiratory collapse or cardiac failure. In each, either the lung or the heart can't take it any more, and give up,

Some researchers claim that sniffing certain chemicals makes the heart fatally vulnerable to adrenaline, a heart-stimulating hormone released during the stress of shocks or scares. If something frightens the sniffer, the adrenaline-sensitized heart fails. Death comes suddenly.

Most people want to know about permanent damage. Does sniffing cause irreversible damage? In prolonged, high doses, yes; in occasional doses, it's unlikely.

Prolonged high doses means industrial contact by workers who are exposed to chemicals every day and in high doses. The workers suffer physical damage and instances of cancer are higher among them than the general population.

Most medical research acknowledges the damage done by the chemicals used by sniffers. Inhalant chemicals do permanent damage in bone marrow, lungs, kidneys, liver, heart, eyes, and brain. In the occasional user, damage of this kind is very rare. For this user, the chances of damage are pretty slim.

For the occasional sniffer, the main problem is with tolerance, which is the need to sniff more to create the same effect. When tolerance increases, the possibilities of abuse do, too. Permanent damage becomes a concern.

The important point here is: Occasional experimental use of most of these vaporous chemicals doesn't pose an inevitable health threat to the user. Instead, focus must be placed on the misuser.

A danger for the misuser is mixing chemicals. For example, sniffing and drinking can combine to create an overpowering punch which has a killing potential. All drugs taken in combination have a dangerous potential. Inhalants are no different. A rule of thumb: Don't mix drugs! Another rule: When stoned, don't drive or operate dangerous machinery! These rules can save a sniffer's life, as well as those he endangers when driving.

What sniffers look like.

Sniffers are not deformed perverts, criminals, or madmen luring in shadows to kill the innocent. These are false images. More that likely, sniffers look quite a bit like our own sons and daughters.

The age span for sniffers is quite wide, though generally the ages range between 10 and 17 years old. Kids as young as 6 and 7 sniff, and adults as old as 20 are known sniffers. But usually inhalants are the first drugs used and their use starts around ages 10 or 11.

In the past, the sniffer was typically a young boy from an impoverished Hispanic-American background. Though sniffers still are young, predominantly male, and usually Hispanic, things are changing. More girls are sniffing, but boys still hold a slight edge in numbers. Recently, more whites are sniffing. Indians, too, are seen more often in the statistics, especially those Indians on reservations and in Indian boarding schools. Black youths still are "under-represented" in the statistics.

That means that inhalants are not their drugs of choice for getting loaded. But recently, more black youths are seen as sniffers, though their numbers are not at the levels of the other groups.

For girls who are either pregnant or at risk of pregnancy, inhalants pose a serious problem. These chemicals, in high doses continually sniffed, cause birth defects and malformations. Though casual sniffing is considerably different, the chance still persists that birth defects can occur. Why take chances?

CHAPTER SIX

Terminology

Some Substances Used for Nonprescribed Drugging Effects

Morphine

SLANG NAME: White Stuff, M.

SOURCE: Natural (from opium)

MEDICAL USE: Pain relief

USUAL FORM OF PRODUCT: Powder (white), tablet, liquid

LONG-TERM POSSIBLE EFFECTS: Addiction, constipation, loss of appetite

PSYCHOLOGICAL DEPENDENCE POTENTIAL: Yes

ACTIVE INGREDIENT: Morphine, sulphate

PHARMACOLOGIC CLASSIFICATION: Central nervous system depressant

HOW TAKEN: Swallowed or injected

EFFECTS SOUGHT: Euphoria, prevent withdrawal discomfort

PHYSICAL DEPENDENCE POTENTIAL: Yes

ORGANIC DAMAGE POTENTIAL: Yes, indirectly

Heroin

SLANG NAME: H., Horse, Scat, Junk, Smack, Scag, Stuff, Harry

SOURCE: Semi-synthetic (from morphine)

MEDICAL USE: None, legally

USUAL FORM OF PRODUCT: Powder (white, gray or brown)

LONG-TERM POSSIBLE EFFECTS: Addiction, constipation, loss of appetite

PSYCHOLOGICAL DEPENDENCE POTENTIAL: Yes

ACTIVE INGREDIENT: Diacetylmorphine

PHARMACOLOGIC CLASSIFICATION: CNS, depressant

HOW TAKEN: Injected or sniffed

EFFECTS SOUGHT: Euphoria, prevent withdrawal discomfort

PHYSICAL DEPENDENCE POTENTIAL: Yes

ORGANIC DAMAGE POTENTIAL: Yes indirectly

Codeine

SLANG NAME: Schoolboy

ACTIVE INGREDIENT: Methylmorphine

SOURCE: Natural (from opium); semi-synthetic (from morphine)

PHARMACOLOGIC CLASSIFICATION: CNS, depressant

MEDICAL USE: Ease pain and coughing

HOW TAKEN: Swallowed

USUAL FORM OF PRODUCT: Tablet, liquid (in cough syrup)

EFFECTS SOUGHT: Euphoria, prevent withdrawal discomfort

LONG-TERM POSSIBLE EFFECTS: addiction, constipation, loss of appetite

PHYSICAL DEPENDENCE POTENTIAL: Yes

PSYCHOLOGICAL DEPENDENCE POTENTIAL: Yes.

ORGANIC DAMAGE POTENTIAL: Yes, indirectly

Cocaine

SLANG NAME: Corrine, Coke, Flake, Crack, Snow, Gold Dust, Bernice

ACTIVE INGREDIENT: Methylester of bezoylecogonine

SOURCE: Natural (from cocoa leaves)

PHARMACOLOGIC CLASSIFICATION: Hallucinogen

MEDICAL USE: Local or topical anesthesia

HOW TAKEN: Smoked or Swallowed

USUAL FORM OF PRODUCT: Powder (white), liquid

EFFECTS SOUGHT: Relaxation, euphoria, increased perception

LONG-TERM POSSIBLE EFFECTS: Depression, convulsions

PHYSICAL DEPENDENCE POTENTIAL: No.

PSYCHOLOGICAL DEPENDENCE POTENTIAL: Yes.

ORGANIC DAMAGE POTENTIAL: Probable.

Marijuana

SLANG NAME: Pot, grass, tea

ACTIVE INGREDIENT: Tetrahydrocannabinols

SOURCE: Cannabis Sativa

PHARMACOLOGIC CLASSIFICATION: Hallucinogen

MEDICAL USE: None

HOW TAKEN: Smoked or swallowed

USUAL FORM OF PRODUCT: Plant Particles (dark green or brown)

EFFECTS SOUGHT: Euphoria, relaxation, increased perception

LONG-TERM POSSIBLE EFFECTS: Usually none. Bronchitis, conjunctivitis, psychosis

PHYSICAL DEPENDENCE POTENTIAL: No.

PSYCHOLOGICAL DEPENDENCE POTENTIAL: Probable.

ORGANIC DAMAGE POTENTIAL: Not determined.

Hashish

SLANG NAME: Hash

ACTIVE INGREDIENT: Tetrahydrocannabinols

SOURCE: Cannabis Sativa

PHARMACOLOGIC CLASSIFICATION: Hallucinogen

MEDICAL USE: None

HOW TAKEN: Smoked or swallowed

USUAL FORM OF PRODUCT: Solid brown to black, resin

EFFECTS SOUGHT: Relaxation, euphoria, increased perception

LONG-TERM POSSIBLE EFFECTS: Usually none. Conjuctivitis, possible.

PHYSICAL DEPENDENCE POTENTIAL: No

PSYCHOLOGICAL DEPENDENCE POTENTIAL: Probable.

ORGANIC DAMAGE POTENTIAL: Not determined.

Dom

SLANG NAME: STP, "Serenity, Tranquility, Peace"

ACTIVE INGREDIENT: 4-Methyl-2, 5- Dimethoxyalpha, Methylphenethy-amine

SOURCE: Synthetic

PHARMACOLOGIC CLASSIFICATION: Hallucinogen

MEDICAL USE: None

HOW TAKEN: Swallowed

USUAL FORM OF PRODUCT: Tablets, capsules, liquid

EFFECTS SOUGHT: Stronger than LSD effects.

LONG-TERM POSSIBLE EFFECTS: Unknown

PHYSICAL DEPENDENCE POTENTIAL: No

PSYCHOLOGICAL DEPENDENCE POTENTIAL: Possible

ORGANIC DAMAGE POTENTIAL: Not determined

THC

SLANG NAME: None

ACTIVE INGREDIENT: Tetrahydrocann-binal

SOURCE: Synthetic

PHARMACOLOGIC CLASSIFICATION: Hallucinogen

MEDICAL USE: None

USUAL FORM OF PRODUCT: In marijuana or liquid

HOW TAKEN: Smoked or swallowed

LONG-TERM POSSIBLE EFFECTS: Unknown

EFFECTS SOUGHT; Stronger than marijuana effects

PSYCHOLOGICAL DEPENDENCE POTENTIAL: Possible

PHYSICAL DEPENDENCE POTENTIAL: No

ORGANIC DAMAGE POTENTIAL: Not determined

DMT

SLANG NAME: Business man's special

ACTIVE INGREDIENT: Dimethyltrpta-maine

MEDICAL USE: None

PHARMACOLOGIC CLASSIFICATION: Hallucinogen

USUAL FORM OF PRODUCT: Liquid

HOW TAKEN: Injected

LONG-TERM POSSIBLE EFFECTS: Unknown

EFFECTS SOUGHT: Shorter term than LSD effects

PSYCHOLOGICAL DEPENDENCE POTENTIAL: Possible

PHYSICAL DEPENDENCE POTENTIAL: No

ORGANIC DAMAGE POTENTIAL: Not determined

Barbiturates

SLANG NAME: Barbs, Red Devils, Yellow Jackets, Phennies, Peanuts, Blue Heaven Candy

ACTIVE INGREDIENT: Phenobarbital, pentobarbital, secobarbital, amobarbital

SOURCE: Synthetic

PHARMACOLOGIC CLASSIFICATION: CNS depressant

MEDICAL USE: Sedation, relieve high blood pressure, epilepsy

HOW TAKEN: Swallowed or injected

USUAL FORM OF PRODUCT: Tablets or capsules

EFFECTS SOUGHT: Anxiety reduction

LONG TERM POSSIBLE EFFECTS: Severe withdrawal symptoms, possible convulsions, toxic psychosis

PHYSICAL DEPENDENCE POTENTIAL: Yes

PSYCHOLOGICAL DEPENDENCE POTENTIAL: Yes

ORGANIC DAMAGE POTENTIAL: Yes

Amphetamines, Methamphetamines

SLANG NAME: Bennies, Dexies, Hearts, Pep Pills, Speed, Lid Propers, Wake-Ups

ACTIVE INGREDIENT: Amphetamine, dextroamphetamine, methamphetamine (desoxyephedrine)

SOURCE: Synthetic

PHARMACOLOGIC CLASSIFICATION: CNS stimulant

MEDICAL USE: Control appetite, narcolepsy, some childhood behavioral disorders

HOW TAKEN: Swallowed or injected

USUAL FORM OF PRODUCT: Tablets capsules, liquid, powder (white)

EFFECTS SOUGHT: Alertness,

LONG TERM POSSIBLE EFFECTS: Loss of appetite, delusions, hallucinations, toxic psychosis

PHYSICAL DEPENDENCE POTENTIAL: Possible

PSYCHOLOGICAL DEPENDENCE POTENTIAL: Yes

ORGANIC DAMAGE POTENTIAL: Probable

LSD

SLANG NAME: Acid, Big D, Sugar, Trips, Cubes

ACTIVE INGREDIENT: D-lysergic acid Diethylamide

SOURCE: Semi-Synthetic (from ergot alkaloids)

PHARMACOLOGIC CLASSIFICATION: Hallucinogen

MEDICAL USE: Experimental research only

HOW TAKEN: Swallowed

USUAL FORM OF PRODUCT: Tablets, capsules, liquid

EFFECTS SOUGHT: Insight, distortion of senses, exhilaration

LONG-TERM POSSIBLE EFFECTS: May intensify existing psychosis panic reactions

PHYSICAL DEPENDENCE POTENTIAL: No

PSYCHOLOGICAL DEPENDENCE POTENTIAL: Possible

ORGANIC DAMAGE POTENTIAL: Not determined

Paregoric

SLANG NAME: None

ACTIVE INGREDIENT: Tincture of Camphorated opium

SOURCE: Natural (from opium) and synthetic

PHARMACOLOGIC CLASSIFICATION: CNS depressant

MEDICAL USE: Sedation, counteract diarrhea

HOW TAKEN: Swallowed or injected

USUAL FORM OF PRODUCT: Liquid

EFFECTS SOUGHT: Euphoria, prevent withdrawal discomfort

LONG-TERM POSSIBLE EFFECTS: Addiction, constipation, loss of appetite

PHYSICAL DEPENDENCE POTENTIAL: Yes

PSYCHOLOGICAL DEPENDENCE POTENTIAL: Possible

ORGANIC DAMAGE POTENTIAL: Yes indirectly

Meperidine

SLANG NAME: None

ACTIVE INGREDIENT: Meperidine Hydrochioride

SOURCE: Synthetic (morphine-like)

PHARMACOLOGIC CLASSIFICATION: CNS depressant

MEDICAL USE: Pain relief

USUAL FORM OF PRODUCT: tablet, liquid

HOW TAKEN: Swallowed or injected

LONG-TERM POSSIBLE EFFECTS: Addiction, constipation, loss of appetite

EFFECTS SOUGHT: Euphoria, prevent withdrawal discomfort

PSYCHOLOGICAL DEPENDENCE POTENTIAL: Yes.

PHYSICAL DEPENDENCE POTENTIAL: Yes

ORGANIC DAMAGE Yes, indirectly.

Methadone

SLANG NAME: Dolly

ACTIVE INGREDIENT: Methadone, Hydrochioride

SOURCE: Synthetic (morphine-like)

PHARMACOLOGIC CLASSIFICATION: CNS depressant

MEDICAL USE: Pain relief

HOW TAKEN: Swallowed or injected

USUAL FORM OF PRODUCT: tablet, liquid

EFFECTS SOUGHT: Prevent withdrawal discomfort

LONG-TERM POSSIBLE EFFECTS: Addiction, constipation, loss of appetite

PHYSICAL DEPENDENCE POTENTIAL: Yes

PSYCHOLOGICAL DEPENDENCE POTENTIAL: Yes.

ORGANIC DAMAGE POTENTIAL: Yes, indirectly.

PCP

SLANG NAME: Hog, Peace Pill

ACTIVE INGREDIENT: Phencyclidine

SOURCE: Synthetic

PHARMACOLOGIC CLASSIFICATION: Hallucinogen

MEDICAL USE: Veterinary anesthetic

HOW TAKEN: Swallowed

USUAL FORM OF PRODUCT: Tablets, capsules

EFFECTS SOUGHT: Harsher than LSD

LONG-TERM POSSIBLE EFFECTS: Unknown

PHYSICAL DEPENDENCE POTENTIAL: No

PSYCHOLOGICAL DEPENDENCE POTENTIAL: Possible.

ORGANIC DAMAGE POTENTIAL: Not determined.

Mescaline

SLANG NAME: Mesc

ACTIVE INGREDIENT: 3,4,5,-trimethox-phenethylamine

SOURCE: Natural (from peyote cactus)

PHARMACOLOGIC CLASSIFICATION: Hallucinogen

MEDICAL USE: None

USUAL FORM OF PRODUCT: Tablet, capsule

HOW TAKEN: Swallowed

EFFECTS SOUGHT: Same as LSD

LONG-TERM POSSIBLE EFFECTS: Unknown

PHYSICAL DEPENDENCE POTENTIAL: No

ORGANIC DAMAGE POTENTIAL: Not determined

PSYCHOLOGICAL DEPENDENCE POTENTIAL: Possible

Psilocybin

SLANG NAME: Magic mushrooms, 'shrooms

ACTIVE INGREDIENT: 3 (2-dimenthyla-mino), ethylindo-4-old-hydrogen phosphate

SOURCE: Natural (from psilocybe) fungus on a type of mushroom

PHARMACOLOGIC CLASSIFICATION: Hallucinogen

MEDICAL USE: None

USUAL FORM OF PRODUCT: tablet, capsule

HOW TAKEN: Swallowed

EFFECTS SOUGHT: Same as LSD

LONG-TERM POSSIBLE EFFECTS: Unknown

PHYSICAL DEPENDENCE POTENTIAL: Not determined

PSYCHOLOGICAL DEPENDENCE POTENTIAL: Possible

ORGANIC DAMAGE POTENTIAL: Not determined.